D0341952

Built by Wendy
DRESSES

TO MRMC

THANKS TO...

Howard Mullin and Joan Frankel, Janis Mullin, Jason and Erin Mullin, Danny Mullin, Sameena Ahmad, Jenny Gossmann, Dana Vaccarelli, Marc Swanson, Erica Smith and Betty Wong at Potter Craft, Rhiannon Kubicka, Marc Gerald at the Agency Group, Beci Orpin and family, Agnieszka Gasparska, Eviana Hartman, Wallace Fludd, Michael Calderone, and John Domingez.

Copyright © 2010 by Wendy Mullin

All rights reserved.

Published in the United States by Potter Craft,
an imprint of the Crown Publishing Group,
a division of Random House, Inc., New York.
www.crownpublishing.com
wwww.pottercraft.com

POTTER CRAFT and colophon is a registered trademark of Random House, Inc.

Library of Congress Cataloging-in-Publication Data

Mullin, Wendy.
  Built by Wendy dresses : the Sew U guide to making a girl's best frock / Wendy Mullin with Eviana Hartman; illustrations by Beci Orpin; additional illustrations by Dana Vaccarelli.
      p. cm.
  Includes bibliographical references and index.
  ISBN 978-0-307-46133-9
  1. Girls' clothing. 2. Dressmaking—Patterns. 3. Dresses. I. Hartman, Eviana. II. Title.
  TT562.M95 2009
  646.4'32—dc22
                          2009027937

Printed in China

10 9 8 7 6 5 4 3 2 1

First Edition

Built by Wendy

DRESSES

THE SEW U GUIDE TO MAKING A GIRL'S BEST FROCK

Wendy Mullin

with Eviana Hartman

ILLUSTRATIONS BY BECI ORPIN

ADDITIONAL ILLUSTRATIONS BY DANA VACCARELLI

POTTER
CRAFT

NEW YORK

CONTENTS

INTRODUCTION 6

FROCKS ROCK: Why Dresses are a Girl's Best Friend—and Fun to Sew, Too

Book Smart: What to Expect

CHAPTER 1 12

DESIGN WITHIN REACH: How to Create the Perfect Dress for You

- Triple Treat: Getting to Know Your New Dress Patterns
- Body Language: Know Your Figure Type
- Small Wonders: Details to Dress Up Your Design
- Dream Weavers: Choosing Dress Fabrics
- Linings: The Inside Scoop
- Bells and Whistles: Trims to Try
- Vision Quest: Considering Design, Shape, and Fabric

CHAPTER 2 28

THE SHAPE OF THINGS: Dress Patterns: How to Make Them, How to Remake Them

- Tool Time: Patternmaking Supplies
- The Large and Small of It: How to Determine Your Size
- On Your Marks, Get Set, Go: Understanding Pattern Markings

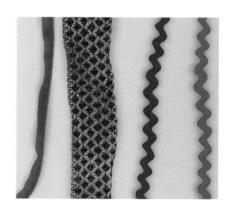

- Shape Shifting: Techniques for Altering Basic Patterns
- Testing, Testing: Making a Muslin
- Altered State: Perfecting Your Patterns
- Your Aim Is True: Finalizing the Pattern

CHAPTER 3 44

SNIP TO IT! Prepping and Cutting Like a Pro

- Tool Time: Cutting Supplies
- Prep School: Getting Fabric Ready to Cut
- Cut! Built by Wendy's Seven Simple Steps for Cutting

CHAPTER 4 52

IN STITCHES: How to Make Sewing Your Dress a Success

- Tool Time: Sewing Supplies
- Equipment: Rise of the Machines
- Sewing Dresses: A Crash Course
- Seams: Easy as 1, 2, 3
- Finish What You Started: Fray-Proofing Seam Allowances
- Secure Stitching: Hold to It
- Living on the Edge: Finishing Raw Openings
- The Heat Is On: Pressing

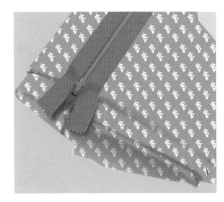

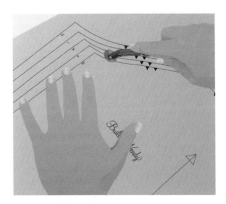

- An Open-and-Shut Case: Buttons and Buttonholes
- Zip, Zip, Hooray: Sewing Zippers
- Pockets: The Inside Story

CHAPTER 5 76

THE SHEATH DRESS

- Pattern Pieces
- Sewing Notes
- Built by You Projects

CHAPTER 6 116

THE SHIFT DRESS

- Pattern Pieces
- Sewing Notes
- Built by You Projects

CHAPTER 7 158

THE DIRNDL DRESS

- Pattern Pieces
- Sewing Notes
- Built by You Projects

CHAPTER 8 201

RECYCLING: From Rags to Dresses

RESOURCES 204

GLOSSARY 205

BIOGRAPHIES 207

INDEX 208

FROCKS ROCK

Why dresses are a girl's best friend—
and fun to sew, too

THERE'S ONE SUREFIRE WAY TO SOLVE A FASHION EMERGENCY: THROW ON A DRESS.

The dress has been the building block of women's wardrobes since the dawn of civilization—it's the quickest, simplest way to cover the body, after all. In fact, until Marlene Dietrich and Katharine Hepburn popularized trousers in the 1930s, it was generally unheard of for women *not* to wear dresses. (Men have worn, and wear, dress-like robes and gowns, too, but I won't be writing a book about those anytime soon.) From Greek togas to Marie Antoinette's corseted crinolines, from Coco Chanel's LBD to Rudi Gernreich's micro-minidresses, from Lizzie Bennet's no-frills frocks in *Pride and Prejudice* to Marilyn Monroe's classic subway-grate scene in white pleats, dresses have reflected the times and captured the imagination throughout history. And they've provided some of the most memorable moments in pop culture (who could forget Björk's swan frock at the Oscars, or a very pregnant M.I.A.'s sheer Grammy dress with strategic polka-dots?).

When I first started sewing my own clothes two decades ago, I focused on dresses. Part of the reason why, of course, was that they were so easy to wear. Back in high school, my allowance didn't get me very far at the mall, and it made more sense to me to wear outfits consisting of one piece of clothing (just add shoes!) than to pony up for a shirt *and* pants. (Then again, my affinity for dresses also had a lot to do with my teenage awkwardness. I dyed my hair so many different colors that at one point it was so fried I had to cut it super-short, à la Mia Farrow in *Rosemary's Baby*. I was also pretty gangly. So dresses ensured that people wouldn't think I was a boy!)

I learned about dresses by dissecting them like science-class specimens. My mom kept a lot of her old clothing in our basement, and she had this sweet Liberty of London floral dress that I cut apart to see how the pattern was made. She wasn't too happy about it, but I figured she wouldn't miss the ruffled prairie skirt with Victorian bodice and leg-of-mutton sleeves. Anyway, the episode taught me a lot about construction. My mom and I have pretty different body shapes—she's busty, I'm not—so anytime I wanted to steal her old stuff, I had to tweak it to fit my shape. I found that basic shift-type dresses were pretty easy to alter to flatter different bodies—a discovery that will serve you well on the following pages. Dresses, you see, have all sorts of features built in to accentuate the female form—to alter the waist-to-hip ratio, to conceal or reveal, to add or subtract. That's why they're so alluring, and so popular.

Once my early sewing experiments evolved past the potato-sack stage, I found that the simple shift silhouette was a great canvas for experimentation. I added rickrack trim to hems, and even covered the entire bodice of one dress in brightly colored heart-shaped buttons! Later, when Built by Wendy first began, I always included plenty of dresses in the line. They were a great blank slate for creativity: With the smallest of changes, I could turn a basic pattern into several wildly different incarnations.

Even now, I generally use pretty simple shapes for the dresses in my collections. I also design fits that can be worn by many body types and take real life into consideration: strap shapes that work if you're wearing a bra, sleeve cuts for those who don't like their upper arms, necklines that are flattering. All of this will come in handy on the following pages, where I'll show you sewing projects for dresses that are a lot less complicated than they look, all based on patterns that I can assure you are flattering—after all, I've spent years talking to my customers about what works and what doesn't!

book smart

Built by Wendy Dresses includes everything you need to design and sew your own dresses, along with all sorts of inspiring tips to get your creative juices flowing. It's targeted to beginning sewers and aspiring designers who want to explore the possibilities of dresses, although more advanced sewers will find plenty to work with. As with my previous books, *Sew U* and *Sew U: Home Stretch*, this book includes three basic patterns in a special sealed envelope. For each style, I've developed several step-by-step projects, where I show you easy ways to customize the basic patterns. Simple adjustments like shortening or lengthening hems, adding or subtracting collars and sleeves, and switching up fabrics and trims will allow you to create a whole range of dress options for every situation, from the beach to black-tie galas. Whether you want to make a basic black dress to show off your jewelry or a festive printed strapless frock with ruffles to show off your design chops, I'll walk you through it.

One really cool feature unique to this book is a special section about fit. Dresses are particularly well suited to the female figure, and each style does different things for different bodies. I'll explain how to assess your shape, and provide suggestions about which dress silhouettes will flatter you the most, whether it's a nipped-in shirtwaist to give a boyish build more definition or a structured shift to streamline curves.

As in *Sew U* and *Sew U: Home Stretch*, I'll include plenty of tips and tricks that you won't find in traditional sewing books, hard-won wisdom based on my two decades worth of experience as a sewer (sometimes on a tight budget, and sometimes knowing very little). I'll go over the basics of setting up a sewing room with supplies and organizing tips; I'll offer up a crash course in sewing and patterns as they relate to the special properties of dresses. However, this book isn't a comprehensive primer on sewing. You'll probably be able to get by if you're fairly new at it, but if you've never so much as laid eyes on a needle before, it's a good idea to have *Sew U* on hand to really get into the nitty-gritty of what patterns, fabrics, cutting, and sewing are all about.

And, back by popular demand, I've included a section of ideas for remaking and recycling old garments into new dresses, including both small hints like salvaging vintage buttons from Granny's hand-me-downs and bigger projects like chopping down your old prom dress into something more casual.

Most of all, this book is meant to inspire you and to teach you to think outside the box (or think outside the box pleat, as the case may be). You can follow my design suggestions, or take them as a starting point and let your imagination run wild. Dresses are arguably the most fun things for a budding designer to make—not to mention the most fun to wear. And, of course, making your own means you'll never get caught sporting the same dress as someone else at a party. So get ready, get set, and let's get dressed!

CHAPTER 1

DESIGN WITHIN REACH

HOW TO CREATE THE PERFECT DRESS FOR YOU

AS A DESIGNER, I HAVE A MANTRA: FLATTERY WILL GET ME EVERYWHERE.

I always begin the process of planning my collections by choosing silhouettes that will work with a variety of body types: small or large hips, an hourglass or boyish figure, a small or large chest. I design for reality, not the runways—I have friends and clients in all shapes and sizes, and, hey, I'm a woman too, and I like clothes to make me look and feel good! Luckily, dresses are incredibly versatile garments. In this book, I have included three basic patterns that I've found look good on most figure types during the two decades I've been making clothes. Believe it or not, these three simple templates are the basis for most of the dress styles in my collections. I use them season after season, because they work!

Then, before I start daydreaming about ruffles and ribbons, I think about practical matters. What season will the dress be worn in, and how will it fit in with my busy life (or, for that matter, make it easier)? For my fall/winter collections, I usually plan a few casual dresses for everyday wear (cute, cozy, rustic pieces to throw on for a walk in the park or museum-hopping) and a few nice dresses that can make the transition from work to early-evening events like art openings (which always seem to pick up around that time of year). I also include some festive, head-turning dresses for cocktail parties and holiday celebrations. When I'm thinking about spring, I think of beach cover-ups, colorful sundresses to toss on with flip-flops for a barbecue or afternoon shopping, and comfortable, lightweight looks for hot, muggy summer nights. You'll want to think about designing this way, too—after all, what good is a mohair sundress if it makes you sweat like crazy on an April afternoon?

Once you have an idea about the kind of dress you want to make, it's time to get creative! In this chapter, I'll give you ideas about how to play with design details like necklines, sleeves, and hem shapes. I'll explain which of these elements work particularly well with the three dress patterns and projects in the book. Fabric and trim are where your imagination really gets to run wild. I'll go over the unique properties of some of the most popular options, and suggest plenty of fun ways to spice things up, from buttons to fringe. And—this is crucial—you'll learn how all these elements (body shape, design elements, fabrics, trims, and colors) can work together to create the cutest, most flattering dresses for you.

triple treat

GETTING TO KNOW YOUR NEW DRESS PATTERNS

In this book I have included three different patterns: the sheath dress, the shift dress, and the dirndl dress. I chose them not only because they complement most body types, but also because they are such versatile starting points for creating a range of dress styles. You won't believe how different each pattern can become! Here's a look at the properties of each one.

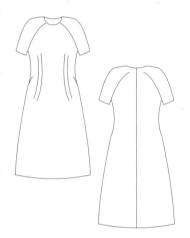

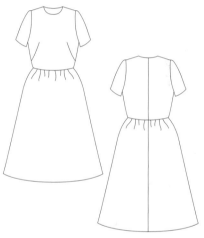

SHEATH DRESS

This basic dress creates some waist definition thanks to front waist darts. The short raglan sleeves make this pattern ideal for adjusting into certain dress shapes that you can't make using a regular set-in sleeve. This shape is great for women with boyish builds who want to create a waist, and also for those with hourglass figures who want to really accentuate the waist.

SHIFT DRESS

This basic pattern does not have any built-in waist definition. The three-quarter-length set-in sleeves and straight body silhouette are ideal starting points for basic patternmaking. Because the structure hovers away from the body, the shift is easy for women with boyish and athletic figures to wear. On curvier figures, it creates a straighter shape, which has an overall slimming effect (and nicely hides lumps and bumps).

DIRNDL DRESS

This pattern has a fitted bodice, a waist seam, and a gathered skirt for a more shapely look. Not only is it great for patternmaking—its unique properties can be adapted to make several dress designs that the other two patterns can't make—but it looks great and fits all figure types. This silhouette is especially great on pear shapes, because the fuller skirt hides hips and draws the eye upward to the waist and torso.

body language

KNOW YOUR FIGURE TYPE

Figure types are based on the ratio between your hips and waist, the width of your shoulders, and your bust size. Most of us know without measuring what type of shape we have (and what we like and don't like about it). The great thing about designing—especially with dresses—is that you can use silhouette to amp up or minimize your proportions. One thing to keep in mind: While all three basic *patterns* in this book offer something for everyone, some of the specific *projects* in this book, because they have specific pattern alterations and design elements, work better with different figures than others. But fear not, budding designers: I will suggest ways you can tweak each project so that every dress in the book can work with your figure type. It's not hard to do!

PEAR

With large hips and a small waist, and usually with narrow shoulders and a smaller bust, this body type is often characterized by more than a 10" (25.5cm) difference between waist and hip measurement. Think J. Lo.

BOY

Slim hips, a straight waist, and an average bust make for a straighter silhouette with less than 10" (25.5cm) difference between waist and hip measurements. Think Keira Knightley.

HOURGLASS

Just like it sounds: a curvy silhouette with a small waist. Hip and waist measurements are usually about 13" (33cm) apart, and this type often has larger bust and shoulder measurements. Think Scarlett Johansson.

ATHLETIC

Also known as the carrot, this body type has a slim waist and hips with broad shoulders and a large bust. Think Angelina Jolie.

AVERAGE

Hips and shoulders are aligned, bust size is neither small nor large, and the difference between hip and waist measurement is right around the standard measurement of 10" (25.5cm).

small wonders

DETAILS TO DRESS UP YOUR DESIGN

There are so many elements that go into a dress, and changing just one of them can result in a totally new look. Here, some pattern details that are a cinch to switch up.

NECKLINES

All of the patterns in the book come with a simple jewel neckline. With a little bit of simple, not-scary-at-all patternmaking, it's easy to change it to another shape. Or, amp up the detail even more by adding a collar. These are a few of my favorite neckline designs, but feel free to invent your own!

Scoop
An elegant way to show off a graceful neck and collarbones.

V-Neck
This can look sporty or sexy, depending on how low you go.

Bateau
Very chic, modest, and structured-looking, à la Audrey Hepburn.

U-Neck
A fresh, interesting alternative to the V, and a great way to show off necklaces.

Square

A bold shape that can look bohemian, innocent, or dramatic, depending on how you design the rest of the dress.

Sweetheart

The most romantic neckline of all, this cut accentuates the bust and adds va-va-voom dressiness to basic shapes.

COLLARS

Convertible

This can take a number of forms, but usually means a collar that can be worn flipped up or down, or left open. Standard shirt collars fall into this category.

Peter Pan

This rounded shape has a sweet, gamine innocence that Parisian starlets (and stylists) like to rock.

Ruffle

Dramatic and dressy, this detail always looks right for night. A ruffle collar can be any size, small to huge.

Mandarin

A narrow stand-up band collar usually found in Asian-inspired and military looks.

Tie

This detail can be narrow or voluminous, long or short, depending on the look you're after.

Chelsea

This extended-V collar—named for the epicenter of swinging-sixties London—has a mod-meets-scholarly vibe that's great for romantic fall looks.

SLEEVES

The patterns included in this book have either set-in sleeves (constructed with shoulder seams and armholes) or raglan sleeves (a simpler, softer construction with a seam that goes from the underarm straight up to the neckline). You can create drastically different looks in a dress by shortening or lengthening the sleeves, changing their shape, or adding cuffs. Here are some options to familiarize yourself with.

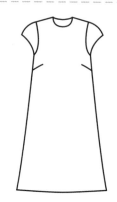

Cap
This tiny, pretty sleeve shape is flattering on most people but not recommended for the broad shouldered (or anyone insecure about her upper arms).

Three Quarter
Also known as bracelet-length, this sleeve length invariably makes the wearer appear chic and graceful. And who doesn't want that?

Types

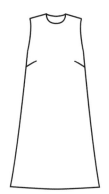

Sleeveless
Going sleeveless isn't just for summer afternoons—just look at Michelle Obama. Sleeveless sundresses are breezier on hot days, of course, but removing the sleeves from a more structured dress can also create a dramatic evening-friendly look (and show off yoga-toned arms).

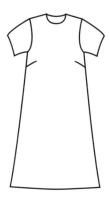

Short
Short sleeves are usually associated with a more casual vibe, but you can also alter the shape to make them drapey and dramatic. Or, use short, straight, T-shirt style sleeves to make a dressy dress (such as a shiny silk shift) less so.

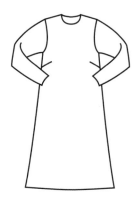

Long
Long-sleeved dresses are lifesavers in winter, but I think it looks cool to make this style in lightweight fabrics (and paired with shorter hems) to play with contrasts. Another fun idea: Try making sleeves super-long for a bit of scrunch at the wrist.

Shapes

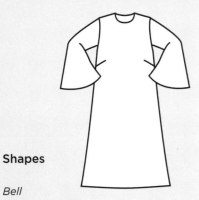

Bell
This looks very different depending on how long you make it: a small flared ruffle, a mid-length angel sleeve, or a groovy, dramatically flared knuckle-duster.

Puff
A versatile sleeve that can look retro-cute when short or romantic when long.

Cuffs

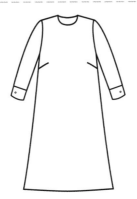

Shirt
The classic button cuff is perfect for day dresses, but could also add a bit of casual cool to a style in fancier fabric (such as silk shantung).

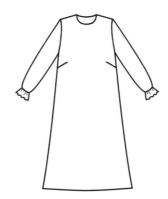

Ruffle
This can add a touch of sweetness to just about any sleeve: Try it with straight, not just gathered, sleeve endings.

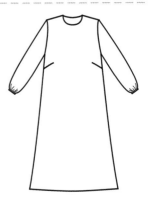

Elastic
Finishing off with elastic will gather a sleeve shape inward for a poufy look.

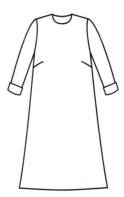

Rolled
Slouchy and cool, this type of sleeve looks great with shirtdresses and other casual daytime looks (you may want to tack it in place or add an epaulet).

HEMS

As I've learned over many years of turning thrift-store muumuus into cute, perfectly fitting frocks, changing the length, width, and shape of dress hems can drastically change the look.

Length

Mini
If you've got it, flaunt it! This is a great length for petite figures and leggy ladies. Minidresses are totally doable for winter (just add wool tights) and dressy events, too.

Classic
Just above the knee is ideal for nearly any situation: work, dinner, meeting the parents.

Tea
Below-the-knee dresses are totally romantic in a 1930s English aristocrat sort of way. They look cool with tall boots or killer heels; try a mermaid-style skirt shape for extra elegance.

Maxi
Hitting near the ankle, this length is formal enough for fancy affairs but it also looks chic for daytime, whether in winter (say, a long, narrow, minimalist wool shift worn with boots beneath) or even high summer (airy hippie-style dresses that billow in the breeze).

Full
For weddings and black-tie events, nothing cuts a more dramatic figure. (Just be sure the length won't trip you up.)

Width

Pencil   A-line   Dirndl

Pencil
Severe, sexy, and chic, a straight skirt shape can also be quite slimming if you choose a structured fabric (which I recommend in most cases anyway to avoid the dreaded visible panty line). If you're very pear shaped, you might want to steer clear—then again, you might want to show off those curves!

A-line
This classic silhouette streamlines curves and allows for movement without adding bulk.

Dirndl
What *is* a dirndl, you ask? It's really just a full, gathered skirt (the name comes from the traditional dress of German peasants). It can be sweeping and romantic at knee-length or longer, or flirty and poufy as a mini.

Shape

Shirt tail
This U-shaped hem dips lower in the front and back and usually is found, as the name would suggest, on shirtdresses.

Banded
A simple band of extra fabric can add contrast to your dress. Add a pop of bold color for a graphic look.

Ruffled
You can add a bottom ruffle to a full skirt for a sexy-señorita vibe or to a straight, stiff pencil skirt to create a flattering, yet polished, mermaid silhouette.

Tunic
This shape is defined by the hem, which has slits on the sides that give dresses an airy look—I like to use it for beach cover-ups. Just be careful if you're making a short mini and plan to wear it sans leggings!

dream weavers
CHOOSING DRESS FABRICS

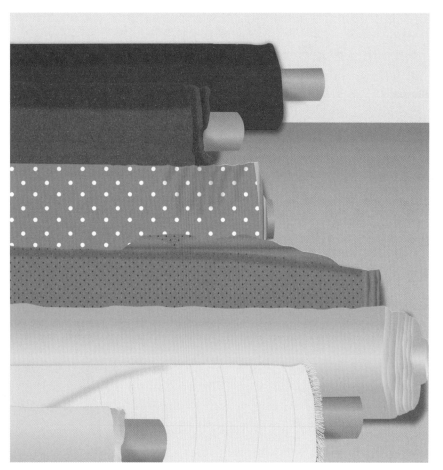

Shopping for fabrics and trims is always the most fun and inspiring part of designing. Some fabrics are easier to work with than others. When I first started sewing, I always made my dresses out of a basic cotton gingham because it was easy to use: The fabric was sturdy and didn't move around a lot, and the grid pattern made it simple to line up patterns and measure detail placement. Now, of course, I create dresses out of everything from slippery silks to sumptuous velvets, solid black fabrics to punchy prints. Here's a list of fabrics I recommend for the dresses in this book.

COTTON

Classic, crisp, and usually casual, cotton is where it's at for warm-weather daytime dresses.

Batiste and Lawn
These lightweight weaves are commonly used for shirts; when making dresses with them, keep in mind that they often need to be lined because they are so sheer.

Broadcloth
This all-purpose, not-too-thin weave is a versatile favorite for spring frocks. Liberty of London florals fall into this category.

Gauze
With a crinkly hand that makes ironing a non-issue, this soft, airy, casual fabric is ideal for summer dresses and bathing suit cover-ups.

Piqué

This finely textured fabric is perfect for preppy summer looks.

Twill and Canvas

These sturdy weaves work for dresses as long as you stick to lighter weights; the stiffer structure means they won't drape as much as some other fabrics, and they'll hover away from the body if you're using a design with volume.

SILK

This elegant family of fabrics will make your new dress look like a million dollars (keep in mind it usually costs a lot more than cotton).

Charmeuse

Beginners, beware: This fluid fabric has a slippery hand that makes it difficult to sew. It's great for fancier dresses, and it's really two fabrics in one: You can make use of the shiny face and matte reverse side to add interest to your design. (I personally like using the matte side out sometimes—the slippery side feels so nice against the skin!)

Chiffon

This sheer silk is dreamy and pretty, but remember to add a more solid layer underneath if you don't want to show off your underwear. It's a nice accent for sleeves and skirt overlays.

Crepe de Chine

Easier to handle than charmeuse, this is a basic matte silk that's ideal for all sorts of dresses.

WOOL

Wool dresses are wonderful in winter. Just be sure not to get something too bulky!

Crepe

A great, drapey basic for making fall dresses warm but not too wooly looking.

Herringbone

Another two-tone pattern fabric with a scholarly, menswear vibe that's fun for fall. Use the lightest weight.

Tweed

This two-tone nubby fabric is fantastic for fall jumpers. Use the lightest weight, and consider adding a lining if it feels itchy.

Voile

Lightweight and drapey, this wool often comes in prints.

BLENDS

Blended fabrics often give you the best of multiple worlds. Wool/silk and cotton/silk blends have a nice drape and feel smooth and luxurious to the touch. A blend containing some man-made fiber (rayon or polyester) might be a good idea if you're worried about wrinkling.

linings
THE INSIDE SCOOP

Dresses hug the body, so depending on what kind of dress you're making, you might need to line it. Anything see-through, itchy, stiff, clingy, or rough against the skin will require some reinforcement. A general guideline: Use lightweight acetate taffeta lining for wools, and use cotton lawn or china silk to line cotton dresses. (Sure, you can skip this step if you're sewing something to wear tonight and you only have a few hours, but with a lining, you'll be a lot more comfortable—and your dress will look a lot more professional. If need be, though, you can always wear a slip or body shaper.) See page 65 for instructions on how to insert a lining.

bells and whistles

TRIMS TO TRY

A little extra something can go a long way when designing a dress. Why not play around with some of these?

CORDAGE, RICKRACK, AND PIPING

This tape is great for outlining curves and seaming details. I like inserting it into front yokes to show off the shape of the yoke.

RIBBONS

I like to topstitch ribbon onto cuffs, collars, and front plackets for a cute, easy detail. Try using striped ribbon on pocket edges or on epaulets of a military-style dress.

CLOSURES

Zippers
Whether regular or invisible, zippers are the most common closure on dresses. Why not use a contrast-color or oversized zipper—or even a zipper stitched on rather than sandwiched in—as an edgy design element?

Snaps
Great to use if you want to hide a closure, snaps come in many sizes. They can also be used as an industrial-chic design element.

Buttons
These can be functional or purely decorative, and come in a variety of sizes, styles, and colors. They're really fun to use as design details—you can use oversized ones, contrast-colored ones, mismatched ones, animal- or heart-shaped ones, vintage ones . . . use your imagination!

DECORATIVE

Lace
I love this for a touch of class on a daytime dress, and it's always de rigueur for evening looks.

Rhinestones
Bust out the BeDazzler! Any plain old dress can be livened up with a burst of faux gems.

Appliqué
Store-bought appliqués can make any dress look more unique, elaborate, and expensive. Try placing them in unexpected places!

vision quest
CONSIDERING DESIGN, SHAPE, AND FABRIC

Now that you are familiar with many of the elements that go into designing a dress, you have to consider how these elements all work together. Sometimes I find a great fabric I love and then I think of a shape it could take, but other times I have a clear vision of a shape I want to make and I have to consider what fabric will work for it.

PRINTS

I love prints, and there's nothing cuter than a colorful dress with a unique print. But you have to really consider the shape and design when working with a print. For instance, if you've chosen a large-scale print, such as a giant floral, I'd advise against making a heavily gathered dress, because the gathers will scramble the print. If a print is very large and bold, you might want to make your dress sleeveless so that you aren't drowning in neon leopard spots.

COLORS

Like print, color needs to be considered in the context of shape. You can use color to draw attention to areas: If you want to show off your arms, you might make the cap sleeves of a dress in a contrasting bright color. On the other hand, drawing attention to a certain area might be the last thing you want. If you prefer to play down your pear shape, don't make a dress with a black bodice and a white, bright, voluminous dirndl skirt!

FABRIC WEIGHT

heavy fabric   light fabric

This is where practicality really comes into play, both in terms of wearing and sewing. I wouldn't advise making the dirndl dress with a gathered skirt in heavyweight wool, for instance, because gathering the fabric will be too tricky. But you don't have to avoid heavier fabric altogether: If you're making the simple shift dress, you might want it to have a boxy shape, in which case a stiffer cotton canvas would have the desired effect. Change the fabric, and the very same pattern can yield two completely different dresses!

CHAPTER 2

THE SHAPE OF THINGS

DRESS PATTERNS: HOW TO MAKE THEM, HOW TO REMAKE THEM

BEFORE A DRESS BECOMES A DRESS, IT STARTS WITH A PATTERN—THE BUILDING BLOCKS OF A GARMENT AS TRANSLATED ONTO PAPER. THIS BOOK, AS I'VE EXPLAINED, INCLUDES THREE BASIC ONES—THE SHEATH, THE SHIFT, AND THE DIRNDL.

Each will serve as a jumping-off point for the projects offered later in the book, as well as any ideas you can dream up yourself!

Fashion designers don't just receive a bolt of inspiration from the heavens, dash off a quick sketch, hit the sewing machine, and—*voilà!*—whip up a new dress. Making a dress without a pattern is kind of like building a house without a blueprint. Sure, there's a chance it might come together, but it's likely to burst at the seams or have corners that don't meet.

Patternmaking, for the purposes of this book, is the process of altering the shape of the three basic patterns to actualize your designs. As I've explained already, sometimes a designer has a clear vision of the silhouette of a garment first, while other times the initial spark of the ideas comes from fabric or trims. Whichever way you get inspired, you'll need to understand the properties of each of the three basic dress patterns included in the book first, which we'll go over in this chapter. Plus, before you start thinking about how to add giant puffed sleeves or dramatic fishtail hems, you need a template for a dress that you can be sure will actually fit you. I'll show you how to choose your size—and how to customize each pattern's fit within that size so that every project in this book works flawlessly with your figure. Once you have all that down pat, you can really get creative, altering the details to create the one-of-a-kind dress of your dreams!

Patterns are delicate and contain a lot of important information, so this chapter will also include some pointers about how to transfer each pattern to regular paper and get it ready for fabric cutting, a process designers call "trueing the pattern."

If you've never encountered a pattern before, it's also a good idea to read *Sew U* for a more in-depth introduction to the world of patterns.

tool time

PATTERNMAKING SUPPLIES

If you're an experienced sewer, chances are you have a fully stocked supply bin already. If you're not, it's important to remember that patternmaking—in addition to the sewing process itself—requires a specific group of tools. Patternmaking takes up a lot of space (on your table and in your brain), and it's best to keep going when you're on a roll, rather than have to run out for an eraser. Think one step ahead, and you'll save time in the long run.

PAPER SCISSORS

Have a pair on hand specifically to cut out your patterns. Your household scissors will work fine, but don't go near your fabric shears—paper will dull them fast. If you live with other people, be sure to label each pair!

CLEAR TAPE

Use this for connecting pattern pieces, especially when folding or slashing and spreading (two techniques I'll explain later).

ROLL OF PAPER

I usually buy a 36" (91cm) wide roll of kraft paper from an art supply store. I use it to transfer the shape of the tissue paper patterns (like the ones included in this book) to a more sturdy, less tear-prone surface.

MEASURING TAPE

This one's a no-brainer: it's essential for measuring your body and finished garments. And no, you're not allowed to use a stiff construction-style tape measure!

PENCIL

When I'm designing, I sketch and erase design lines over and over again. It's best to start fresh with several sharpened pencils that have clean, working erasers.

18" (45.5CM) CLEAR RULER

This is the most important patternmaking tool, in my opinion. It's essential for adding the proper seam allowances to all basic patterns.

WEIGHTS

You'll need something to hold down your basic patterns while transferring them to sturdier paper. Anything from soup cans to paperweights will do the trick.

TRACING WHEEL

This helps to trace lines and curves while you're transferring patterns.

FRENCH CURVE

If you have an even slightly unsteady hand, grab this specialty tool: It works wonders for tracing rounded parts like necklines and armholes.

the large and small of it

HOW TO DETERMINE YOUR SIZE

MEASURE YOURSELF

To determine which size you'll be in the patterns provided in this book, you must first measure three specific points: the bust, waist, and hips. Because this is a beginner-friendly book, we won't get much more detailed than that. If you can find a friend to help you with measuring, all the better—that way, you can make sure your measuring tape isn't off-kilter.

It's not uncommon for women to wear one size on top and another on the bottom—in fact, it happens more often than not. For shirts, the most important measurement is your bust; for skirts and pants, it's the waist and hip measurements. Dresses, however, have to fit you in both places. If your upper and lower body areas are drastically different in size, choose the dress size that fits your bust best, then add or subtract width to the lower half of the dress (which is usually easier to work with than the top half). Later, I will show you how to slightly alter your patterns to fit correctly in all the right places, wherever the imbalance may be.

TIP:

There are three basic patterns included in this book. Familiarize yourself with their components first, and then have a peek at the project chapters for more ideas on how to switch them up and deck them out.

Sheath

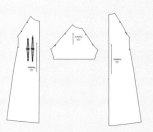

Shift

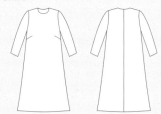
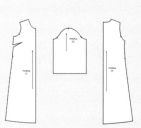

Dirndl

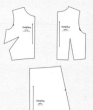

Bust

Measure around the fullest part of your bust.

Waist

Measure your natural waist—that is, the smallest part of your waist. You might want to use a mirror and tie a string around your waist first to find the most accurate point.

Hip

Measure the fullest part of your hip—usually about 7" to 9" (18cm–23cm) below your natural waistline.

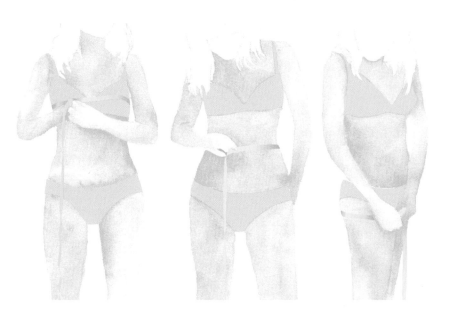

MEASUREMENT CHART

	XS	Small	Medium	Large	XL
Bust	32"–33" (81cm–84cm)	34"–35" (86cm–89cm)	36"–37" (91cm–94cm)	38"–39" (96cm–99cm)	40"–41" (101cm–104cm)
Waist	25"–26" (63cm–66cm)	27"–28" (68cm–71cm)	29"–30" (74cm–76cm)	31"–32" (79cm–81cm)	33"–34" (84cm–86cm)
Hip	35"–36" (89cm–91cm)	37"–38" (94cm–96cm)	39"–40" (99cm–101cm)	41"–42" (104cm–107cm)	43"–44" (109cm–112cm)

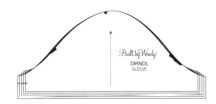

HANDLE WITH CARE: MEET YOUR PATTERN PIECES

Pull out the folded patterns from the envelope. Once you've unfolded them, you'll see each style in a "nested" layout, in which all the sizes are placed on top of each other on the same sheet. Iron the folds out of each piece of paper (not on high heat!) and cut the areas for each of the pattern pieces apart. Stack all of the pieces for each style together, and store them this way—you don't want to discover three weeks from now that you're missing a sleeve piece!

on your marks, get set, go

UNDERSTANDING PATTERN MARKINGS

Before you can test out the patterns to make sure they fit properly, it's important to know what the different pattern markings mean.

LIVING ON THE EDGE: SEAM ALLOWANCES

Most patterns include *seam allowances*: a small addition in overall width to the pattern, usually around ⅝″ (15mm) on commercial patterns, which is the difference between the line where you cut the fabric and the line along which you sew the seam. Put differently, the seam allowance is the space that turns into the leftover fabric on the inside of the seam when you're done sewing.

DARTS

These markings, common in dress patterns, are tucks sewn into the body of the garment to create contours and dimension where fabric would otherwise hang straight. On a pattern, they look like pie slices. Each line is called a dart leg.

NO ALLOWANCE FOR YOU!

The patterns in this book do *not* have seam or hem allowances, unlike the patterns in *Sew U*. Why? This makes it simpler to cut them apart and play around with them without having to sort out where the allowances are and where they've been cut off. For dresses, which can get complicated, it's a better place to start—trust me. (Basic patterns without seam allowances used for the purpose of patternmaking are sometimes called *slopers*.)

What does this mean? Before you cut fabric for the projects in this book, **you'll have to add a seam allowance along the pattern pieces** to allow for the portion of the seam that is inside the garment. I'll remind you about this step for each project later in the book, but it should be committed to memory, especially if you plan to create your own projects using the basic patterns. I generally think ⅝″ (15mm) seam allowances are too big, especially around curved seams, where they tend to get bunchy. Sure, the seams can be trimmed down after sewing, but why complicate things? I prefer to add ½″ (13mm) allowance on most seams and ¼″ (6mm) around small, curved areas such as necklines. For hem allowances it is up to you depending on the style you want, the fabric weight and style, and whether you are inserting a trim into the hem. But generally hems are 1″ to 1½″ (2.5cm–3.8cm).

NOTCHES

These small tapered slits appear along the edges of the seam allowance, but never inside the body of a pattern. Notches appear on the slopers (basic patterns), but you must transfer each notch to the same position on the outer edge of the seam allowance once you add it. Notches can signify many things:

- They can be snipped in matching places on different pieces to indicate which seams are to be sewn together.

- They mark where the legs of a dart begin.

- They mark gathering points, such as the point where the two folds of a pleat meet.

- They mark front and back pieces: Usually, a double notch (2 notches placed ¼″ to ½″ [6–13mm] apart) signifies

the back piece. So on a dress bodice, for instance, there will be a single notch marking the armhole for the front piece and a double notch marking the armhole on the back piece. Then, on the sleeve cap piece, which is sewn to both the front and back armholes, you'll find both single and double notches. Simply line up each type of notch, and you'll know where to sew the pieces together.

GRAIN LINES

The grain of a fabric refers to the lengthwise and crosswise threads of the weave. The grain lines marked on my patterns are there to help you line up the pattern pieces properly. The lengthwise lines marked should run parallel to the fabric's selvage edge (see the illustration explaining grain lines and selvage in Chapter 3, on page 48).

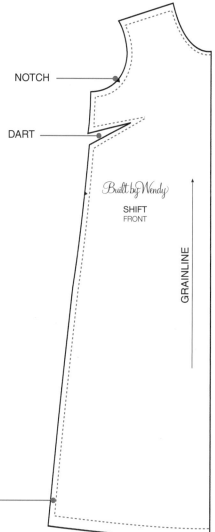

NOTCH

DART

Built by Wendy

SHIFT
FRONT

GRAINLINE

SEAM ALLOWANCE

shape shifting

TECHNIQUES FOR ALTERING BASIC PATTERNS

Changing the fit of basic patterns isn't always about simply drawing a new line. Dress patterns are all about proportion, and the pros use special methods to keep that intact. Plus, there are special ways to handle the patterns themselves while you're doing this. Read on for some patternmaking techniques favored by the pros.

TRANSFERRING PATTERNS TO PAPER

If you're making any alterations whatsoever to your basic pattern—

which, as I've recommended, should itself be transferred to kraft paper for durability—it's best to trace the original pattern piece onto new paper using a tracing wheel. That way, you can play all you want with the copied piece, and if all that messing around makes you mess up, the original hasn't been ruined. Once you've finished, you'll have a complete new pattern just for that dress—which may spawn its own variations (each of which should be copied before altering, natch).

add to seams

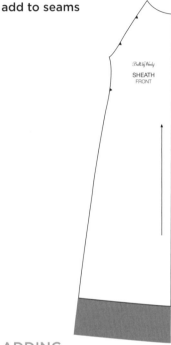

ADDING

To make a garment wider or longer, you can either add to the seams or you can use the slash-and-spread method. Let's say you want to add 2″ (5cm) to the length of your dress. You can simply use your ruler to trace the hem line 2″ (5cm) below where it was onto a new piece of paper (use tape or a weight to hold the sloper down) and then extend the seam lines downward with your pencil, taping the new piece to the old. Or, to use the slash-and-spread

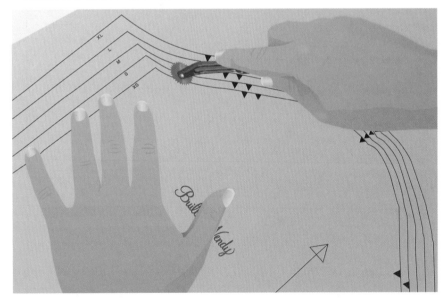

slash and spread

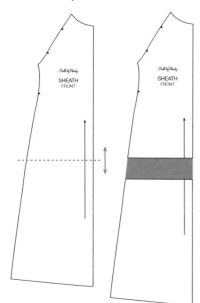

technique, make a slash line across the center of the pattern, cut along the line, and spread the pattern pieces 2" (5cm) apart on top of more paper. Then, tape them down and connect the pieces with pencil lines along the side seams. If you want to make a skirt or bodice or sleeve wider, the same techniques apply. What's the difference? Slashing and spreading keeps the outer seams of the pattern piece intact, so it's a wise choice if you want to keep a garment's shape exactly the same.

SUBTRACTING

Similarly, you can make your dress length shorter by simply cutting off 2" (5cm) across the hem. Or, you can use a technique called folding where you draw a line in the center of the pattern then another line 2" (5cm) above it and fold the pattern so the lines are together. Use a pencil and ruler (curved or straight) to smooth out the resulting line. The same goes for making a skirt or bodice narrower, a sleeve shorter, and so on. Folding will preserve the proportion of the piece more precisely; it's up to you which technique you prefer to use. A sleeve or skirt with a distinct shape, for instance, might look different if you simply cut it off; folding will remove the length or width from within the body rather than along the edge.

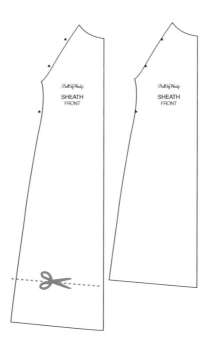

cutting off

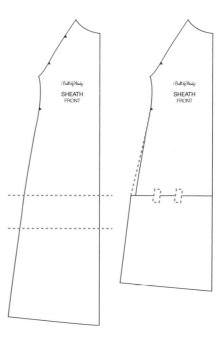

folding

testing, testing
MAKING A MUSLIN

Even once you've measured yourself carefully and cut out the correct pattern size, it's still a good idea to test out the fits of the three patterns first before you go off and do all these projects only to realize they don't fit right. Women's bodies are complicated, and because dresses are designed to flatter them, this step is particularly important for the basic patterns in this book. A muslin is a test garment—usually made of low-cost cotton muslin, hence the name—that allows designers to calibrate a garment's fit without wasting expensive fabric.

1. Trace each of the basic patterns onto paper.

2. Add seam allowances. (Don't bother with hems and necklines, as you won't need to finish them on the muslin and therefore they won't need seam allowances.)

3. Cut out the final patterns.

4. Lay the patterns onto the muslin fabric and cut out each piece.

5. Stitch or pin the pattern pieces together, leaving the seam allowances unfinished (since you won't be wearing the muslin, don't waste your time finishing the raw edges).

6. Try on the muslin and note where anything is too tight, too loose, too long, or too short so that you can adjust the basic patterns accordingly (read on for some ideas).

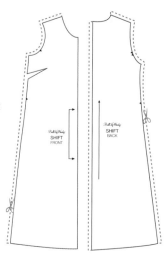

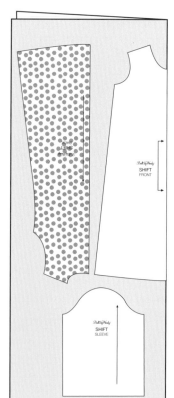

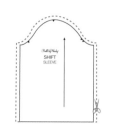

altered state

PERFECTING YOUR PATTERNS

The patterns in this book are based on real Built by Wendy patterns that are, in my experience, flattering to most people. But women's bodies aren't cut from a pattern, and therefore no pattern can fit absolutely everyone everywhere. What to do if your muslin isn't quite right? Here are some ideas, using the adding and subtracting techniques we've just gone over.

The muslin is too tight in the hips:
1. With the dress still on, take a pair of scissors and (carefully!) slash the muslin dress from hem to belly button along the center of the front skirt.

2. Measure the distance that the fabric spreads apart at the hips.

3. Divide that measurement by 4 and, on your pattern, add that amount to each side seam at the hip. Blend a new seam line from that point, going up to the waist and down to the side seam.

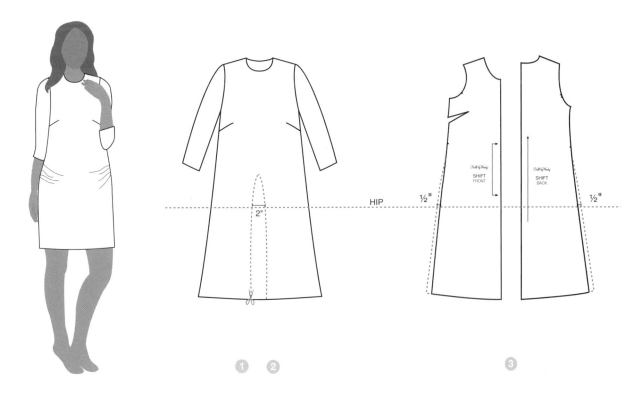

The muslin is too tight in the chest:
1. Using scissors, carefully slash the dress from just below the neck to the belly button in the center front.

2. Measure the distance that the fabric spreads apart at the bust.

3. Divide that measurement by 4 and, on your pattern, add that amount to each side seam from the armhole and blend a new seam line down to the waist.

4. Add that same measurement to the sleeve side seams as well, and blend. You must make sure that the sleeves fit into the new armholes!

The muslin is too loose:

1. Pin the dress along the side seams where you want to tighten the fit. If you have to unpin the muslin to get it off, use chalk, crayon, or a pen to mark where the new pins go before you remove them. Also helpful: Draw a line connecting the pins to get a good idea of the path your new seam lines should follow.

2. Remove the amount pinned from the pattern seams, and draw new seam lines.

The muslin is too long:

1. Pin the sleeves or the hem to the correct length. Have a friend help you if you're shortening a hem, if possible. Otherwise, mark the spot with chalk and take the dress off to pin it, then try it on again to be sure.

2. Subtract that amount from the basic pattern by shortening or folding the pattern piece.

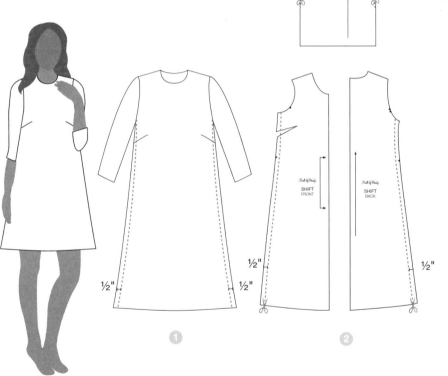

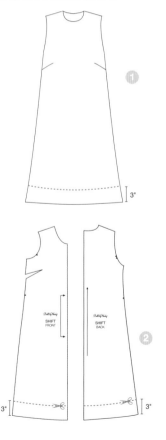

The muslin is too short:

1. Measure from the dress's edge to the ideal position where you would like the sleeve or hem to end. Again, this is usually easier to do with someone helping you.

2. Add that amount to the basic pattern by lengthening or slashing and spreading.

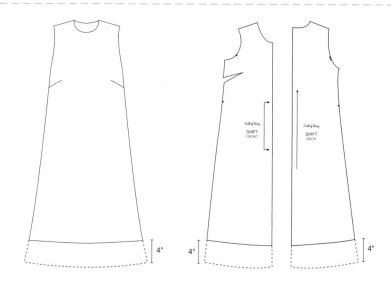

The length proportion of the muslin isn't right (for instance, you're tall and long-waisted and the waistline of the dress hits your ribcage, or you're petite and the bust hits too low):

Measure the distance that the waist and bust are off, and use the slash-and-spread or folding technique to ensure that the waist and bust land in the correct position for your body. In this case, simply adding and subtracting to the pattern isn't a good idea, because that will change the shape and proportion of the bodice and give the waistline a different measurement.

your aim is true
FINALIZING THE PATTERN

Note: The hems on the projects in this book run the gamut from mini to maxi, but the *basic* patterns as I've provided them are supposed to fit as follows:

- The sheath dress pattern has cap sleeves and hits just at the knee

- The shift dress has three-quarter sleeves and hits above the knee

- The dirndl dress pattern hits just below the knee.

Each project in the book has pattern alterations with specific measurements based on these fits, so remember this if you make any permanent changes to the basic patterns. For example, if you strongly prefer short skirts and decide to alter the basic sheath pattern into a mini-length dress pattern upon which all your sheath dress projects will be based, enter that into your calculations when you decide to make a minidress sheath project (which will tell you to remove a few inches from the length). Otherwise you will end up with a top instead!

BACK TO BASICS: MAKING A SLOPER SET

Once you have made changes to your pattern, transfer it (again!) to a fresh sheet of paper by tracing around the edges using your pencil. Now you have created your perfect sloper set, which will form the basis for every dress you make. You can also transfer these onto poster board so they last longer (which I highly recommend). Then, each time you begin a new project, simply trace around the sloper pieces, make your alterations, and then true your pattern (see the next step).

TRUE STORY: TRUEING PATTERNS

To true your pattern, draw the seam allowances by marking points along the outside of the pattern using your clear ruler, and connect them following the shape of the pattern. Use your tracing wheel to transfer the grain lines and other markings to the new pattern piece. Label and cut out each piece. Now, your pattern is ready to be laid onto fabric for cutting and sewing.

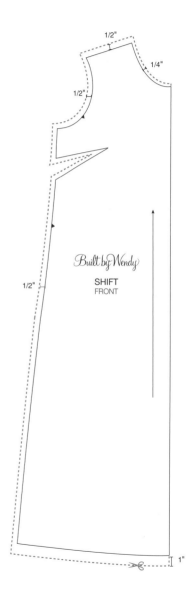

1/2"

1/4"

1/2"

1/2"

1/2"

Built by Wendy

SHIFT
FRONT

1"

CHAPTER 3

SNIP TO IT!

PREPPING AND CUTTING LIKE A PRO

ONCE YOU'VE GOT YOUR PATTERN DOWN PAT, YOU'RE READY TO MAKE THE CUT—THE LAST STEP BEFORE SEWING.

But there's more to cutting than that super-satisfying feeling of slicing into fresh fabric.

Everything from preparing the fabric to placing the pattern pieces must be done methodically, or you'll risk making a mistake and having to buy new fabric (if it hasn't sold out!) or discover that your new dress has downsized to a tank top in the washing machine. I've said it in my other books, and I'll say it again: Think twice, cut once!

A word to beginners: My first book offers an extensive guide to cutting, so I've written this chapter as more of a refresher course. The most important points are included here, but if you've never sewed before, I highly recommend reading *Sew U*, too.

tool time
CUTTING SUPPLIES

A word to the wise: Make sure you have these essentials on hand before you get down to business.

FABRIC SCISSORS

Consign your cheap orange-handled pair to the kitchen junk drawer, and go for a nice pair of stainless steel shears from a brand like Gingher. I suggest the 8″ (20.5cm) size for general use and comfort. You will feel the difference, and they'll last you a lifetime. Just don't use them on paper or anything that's not fabric!

WEIGHTS

Use these to hold down the patterns while you are transferring them to paper and cutting the fabric. If you sew often, you may want to invest in some heavy weights made specifically for patternmaking, but you can get by with a few heavy office objects like a pencil holder or stapler, or even soup cans or some flat washers from the hardware store.

PINS

Sometimes, when fabric is a bit slippery—silk charmeuse is a prime example—it helps to actually pin the pattern to the fabric in the seam allowance, then cut. I prefer colorful plastic-head pins because they're easier to spot, but regular tailor pins work just as well. To pick up scattered pins from the ground or table, use a magnet.

WASHABLE MARKERS

These are great for marking the tips of darts or pocket placement corners. Just be sure to test out the marker on a scrap of your fabric and make sure it can wash out before you cause any permanent damage to your new dress! You can also use a pin for marking points on fabric, if you prefer, but don't do this with delicate fabrics, or you'll create a hole that won't recover.

prep school
GETTING FABRIC READY TO CUT

DOWNSIZE THIS: PRESHRINKING

I can't stand when I wash and dry something and it shrivels up so much that I can't wear it again. There's nothing more frustrating than seeing your favorite cotton dress turned into a top. I've even had to hand down some shrunken items to my friends' teenage kids! Before I make a dress out of cotton fabric, I always wash and dry the fabric as I would when doing a load of laundry at home. Once it's ready, I trim all the frayed edges and iron the fabric back into shape. (Because cotton shrinks, it's smart to buy a little extra when you're calculating yardage for your dress.) Most other fabrics, like wool and silk, are dry-clean only, so there's no need to worry about preshrinking; you may want to dry-clean the fabric first, though, if you're really being cautious.

FACE IT: LEARNING TO TELL FABRIC'S RIGHT FROM WRONG

Most fabrics have a right side and wrong side. The right side is the "face" of the fabric, and the wrong side is the "back." You must always determine which side is the face, and make sure you cut accordingly; few things are more frustrating, or more easily preventable, than a dress with one sleeve that's a slightly different texture than the other! With prints, the face is easy to find, but in some fabrics it's more difficult to discern. Hold the fabric up to bright light, inspect it carefully, and decide which side looks more appealing. If it's a twill, the diagonal lines should be on the front; if it's a silk charmeuse, then the face is the shiny side. Sometimes a textile's brand label will be printed continuously along the selvage edge, which will indicate the face for you. Of course, sometimes you'll want to use the wrong side as a design element, whether it's for texture reasons (as in putting the slippery side against the skin)

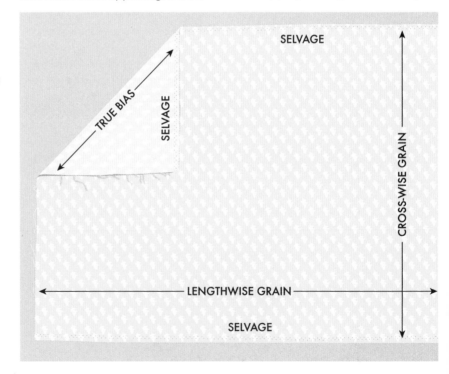

or an accent (like reversing the face for pockets to add a subtle bit of contrast).

CAN I ASK FOR DIRECTIONS?

Some fabrics have a specific direction. With prints you can usually see if it's a "one-way" design (arrows or shapes pointing in one direction, stripes, or words) as opposed to an all over design that looks the same tilted different ways, like a random mini-floral. If you're going to work with a one-way print, be sure to buy extra fabric, because you'll need to lay all the pattern pieces in the same direction. Otherwise, you'll end up with a dress with the front upside down and the back right side up. Other fabrics, such as corduroy and velvet, have a nap—meaning the yarns lay smoother in one direction and coarser in the other. Light hits the directions of napped fabric in different ways, so it's important to cut all the patterns pieces in the same direction. Otherwise, one side of your dress will appear darker and the other lighter.

MATCH POINTS: PLAIDS, STRIPES, AND PATTERNS

When placing pattern pieces on any of these types of fabrics, line up the notches and the bottom edges of the pattern pieces along the horizontal lines. This way, each piece will display the print at exactly the same angle—straight!

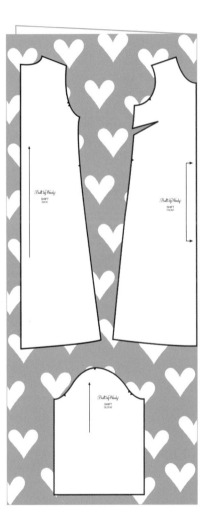

cut!

BUILT BY WENDY'S SEVEN SIMPLE STEPS FOR CUTTING

STEP 1: FOLD

Fold the fabric in half, selvage to selvage and face to face. The face of the fabric should be folded on the inside, so that any markings you make will be on the wrong side of the garment. (If you're using one-way or napped fabric, don't fold it. Follow the instructions for those fabrics instead.)

STEP 2: LAY, LADY, LAY

Lay the pattern pieces on the fabric. Try to place the pieces as close together as possible, but make sure you can fit them all. See the project chapters for recommended layouts for the dress ideas in this book.

> **TIP:**
> Double-check that all patterns cut "on the half" are placed on the fold—this usually means all of the front pieces, since the backs of dresses usually have two pieces.

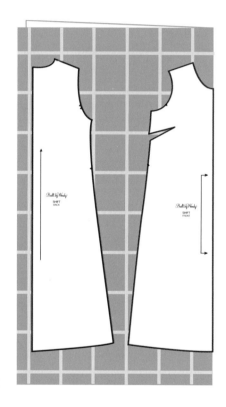

STEP 3: SECURITY CHECKPOINT

Place weights all over the pattern pieces to hold the fabric in place. You can also use pins to secure corners, but this is time-consuming. If you have the hang of cutting, you'll probably just use a combination of weights and your fingers to hold down the pieces as you cut. When using pins, always insert each pin into the seam allowance area of the pattern, rather than inside the seam line, to avoid damaging the fabric.

STEP 4: CHOP, CHOP

Cut the pieces out slowly and carefully—but remember, think twice, cut once.

> **TIP:**
> Make sure that all patterns are placed on the grain. To do this, measure from the selvage to the grain line, down along the grain line, to make sure that the placement runs parallel to the selvage.

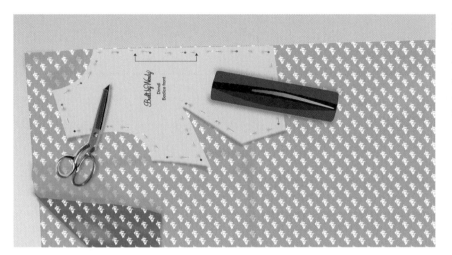

STEP 7: LABELS MATTER

If I know I won't be sewing a style for a while, I always attach a little card to the bundle with the name or a quick sketch of the design so that I remember what to do with it later.

STEP 5: ON YOUR MARKS

Using the tip of your scissors, clip any and all notches into their designated seam allowance areas, being careful not to cut past the seam line into the body of the garment. For darts and pocket placement markings, use a washable pen, tailor's chalk, or pins—whatever you've tested to prove it won't damage the fabric—to mark the area.

STEP 6: BUNDLE UP

If you're not planning to sew your dress right away, make sure you keep all your carefully cut pieces organized for storage. With the pattern pieces still on top of their corresponding cut fabric pieces, stack each piece neatly and roll the entire dress up like a burrito. Tie the bundle together with a ribbon or rubber band, and stow it in a safe place—the last thing you want is your mischievous dog destroying all of your hard work!

CHAPTER 4

IN STITCHES

HOW TO MAKE SEWING YOUR DRESS A SUCCESS

WHEN YOU'RE DOING IT RIGHT, SEWING CAN BE SO SOOTHING. ONCE YOU'VE PREPPED AND CUT YOUR FABRIC PROPERLY, THERE'S SOMETHING ABOUT THE WHIR OF THE MACHINE AND THE FORCE OF THE FEED DOGS THAT'S TOTALLY ZEN.

I can really get into a zone when I'm sewing, but if you haven't prepared everything properly, sewing can bring on stress instead of relieving it. But hey, no worries: In this chapter I'll show you important pointers that we'll use for the book projects, ideas specifically helpful for sewing the types of seams, trims, and other components commonly found on dresses.

This book is a companion volume to the *Sew U* series, so as with the other how-to chapters in this book, I've written this sewing guide more as a series of brush-up pointers than a comprehensive, hand-holding how-to for needle neophytes. If you've never sewed so much as a button before, I strongly encourage you to read *Sew U* first, and get your feet wet making a few practice muslins with your machine before you break out the silk crepe.

tool time
SEWING SUPPLIES

NEEDLES

The projects in this book will mostly rely on machine needles. What kind depends on what you're making: Buy needles compatible with your brand of machine that are the right kind for the weight and type of fabric you'll be using (knit fabrics, for instance, require a special shape of needle; so do denim and leather). It's also good to pick up a small variety pack of basic hand needles, which you'll use to attach buttons. The most popular type is known as sharps, and a package of sizes 1 through 10 should serve most purposes.

THREAD

Thread comes in a dizzying array of thicknesses and materials. You'll find cotton, polyester, silk, and all sorts of combinations. For the projects in this book, you can use an all-purpose mercerized-cotton-wrapped polyester thread. As a general rule of thumb, use heavier thread for heavier fabrics and lighter-weight thread for more delicate fabrics. If you're having a tough time matching thread color to fabric color, always opt for the slightly darker shade. Sometimes it looks cool to use a completely different thread color for contrast—I've made black dresses with white thread, for instance.

SCISSORS

Sure, you can use shears, but small embroidery scissors are so much nimbler for clipping threads as you sew and snipping open buttonholes. Many sewing stores sell pretty, stork-shaped gold ones—I have them, and I love them!

STRAIGHT PINS

Unless you're a world-class whiz on the machine, you'll probably use pins to hold pieces of fabric together while sewing them together. Straight pins vary in size and length, and it's really a matter of personal preference. The most common variety is #17 dressmaker pins. I like ball-head pins because they're colorful, and the little ball on the end is a cinch to handle. Plus, they're easier to spot than the flat-head variety when you drop them on the floor—important to remember if you have carpeting!

SEAM RIPPER

You'll be surprised by how much you use this tool. In fact, I suggest buying two or more to have extras on hand in case one goes missing. For some reason, I always seem to sew sleeves into the wrong armhole, so I'd be lost without mine!

equipment
RISE OF THE MACHINES

CONVENTIONAL SEWING MACHINE

A basic sewing machine is all you'll need to make the projects in this book—just make sure you have one that can operate in reverse and make buttonholes. Whatever type of machine you have, remember to keep it clean and oiled. It's a delicate and sometimes expensive piece of motorized equipment, so take care of it from time to time, as you would your car! Be sure to read the instruction manual for your machine to understand all the settings and capabilities, and keep it in a safe place in case you need to consult it later. (Sometimes you can find these online in PDF format, but don't count on it.) New machines these days are very impressive and usually computerized, so pesky tasks like manually balancing tensions are fast becoming a thing of the past.

SERGER

This machine is often used for knits—the topic of *Sew U: Home Stretch*—but it can also be used to cover the raw edges of seam allowances as you sew. If you don't have one, you can also finish seams with a zigzag stitch on a regular machine or with pinking shears (scissors that cut a zigzag line) so that they don't unravel.

IRON AND BOARD

A strong, clean steam iron is essential for any sewing project. You'll use it to prepare your fabric and press open seams during the sewing process, creating a finished dress that looks professional and flattering. I suggest getting the best one you can afford; your miniature travel iron isn't going to cut it, nor will an old one with crusty melted polyester fused to the surface.

Ironing boards make ironing easier, preserve your tabletops, cut down the risk of burning, and create another work area—and the more surfaces you have to work with, the better. Make sure the cover is clean, or you'll end up pressing old stains onto your new shirt! Before I had an ironing board, I would spread towels on my floor and use them as an ironing surface. Pressing hams—which come in funny shapes designed to help press open curved seams in areas of contour and volume—are nice to have around for making dresses, if you'll be making them often enough to justify spending a little extra.

sewing dresses
A CRASH COURSE

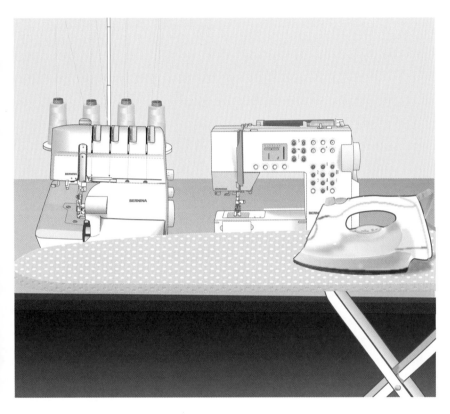

I'm going to go back to my building-a-house analogy here (hey, I call my label Built by Wendy). Like putting up a building, it's easiest to think of sewing a dress as a two-step process. First you have to do the construction so that it's held together and stable—to build a house, that means framing walls and floors; in this case, that means creating seams (attaching parts together) and finishing the raw edges (preventing seam allowances from unraveling, creating hems, encasing with binding, and so on). After that come the details: building in doors and windows or creating closures like buttonholes, adding decorations, and the like. Read on for some useful techniques targeted toward the projects in this book (and, again, read *Sew U* if you're a total newbie).

seams

EASY AS 1, 2, 3

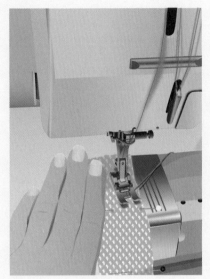

SIMPLE STEPS FOR SEWING A SEAM

Step 1: Ready . . .
Place the pieces to be sewn together with their right sides together. That phrase, which will pop up often in the project chapters, means that the face of the fabric is "kissing" the face of the other piece. (This setup is also sometimes called "face to face.")

Insert the pins into the area that is part of the seam allowance (remember that ½" [13mm] you added to your pattern pieces?). The pins should be perpendicular to the seam so that they're easy to pull out as you sew.

Step 2: Set . . .
Making sure that your machine and bobbin are properly threaded, pull out a finger length of the top thread and the bobbin thread, and place them behind the raised presser foot. Place the fabric pieces under the presser foot along the seam allowance guide marked ½" (13mm).

Step 3: Sew!
Lower the presser foot. Sew a few stitches in the reverse direction to secure the stitching (this is called backstitching; consult your machine's manual if you can't find the reverse switch) and then proceed forward. Once you get to the end, stitch in reverse for about ¼" (6mm) to secure the end. Clip the loose threads with scissors.

DANGEROUS CURVES

Curved seams make dresses fit like a glove, but handling them requires a bit of a learning curve. In any curved seam, one piece of fabric will curve inward and one will curve outward. Because of this, the seam allowances will cause trouble once the seam is sewn. On the inward curve, the allowance will bunch up, and on the outward curve, it will be stretched for space. The solution? Scissors. Once you have stitched each piece just inside the seam allowance, clip (for inward curves) or notch (for outward curves) at regular intervals from the edge to the staystitch. This will create space for overlapping fabric on the inward curve and open up space on the outward curve.

ROLLING WITH THE BUNCHES: GATHERED SEAMS

When making dresses, you'll often have to gather up a larger amount of fabric and stitch it into a smaller space; this is the basic principle of a gathered seam. Puffed cap sleeves and dirndl skirts are two places where you'll use this technique.

1. Set your machine stitch length to the longest option.

2. Sew a row of stitching ¼" (6mm) away from the raw edge, then another ⅜" (9mm) away from the first row.

3. Pull the bottom threads (those that came from the bobbin) and, using your fingers, slowly push the fabric along the threads so it gathers.

4. Pin this gathered piece to the appropriate piece of flat fabric (the bodice or waistband if you're making a gathered skirt, for instance) with the right sides together. Maneuver the gathers to fit into the space evenly.

5. Using a regular-length stitch, sew a seam in between the gathering rows you stitched before, positioning this new seam closer to the second row—about ½" (13mm) from the raw edge.

6. Remove the second row of thread, which will be showing through on the garment. The first row of thread is now encased inside the seam allowance.

finish what you started

FRAY-PROOFING SEAM ALLOWANCES

After you sew each seam, you must finish the raw edge of the seam allowance. This prevents it from unraveling and making a mess of your dress!

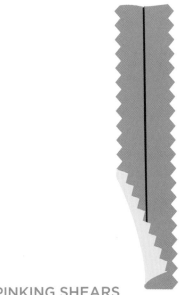

SERGER

Using a serger to seal raw edges with stitching is the fastest, easiest, and most professional way to finish a seam. That is, once you thread this complicated beast!

PINKING SHEARS

This method is a bit old-fashioned, but cutting a zigzag line with these shears is a cheap, fast, and easy way to take care of seam allowances' raw edges. Over time, even these edges will fray a bit, but you can always use a little bit of Fray Check (a liquid sealant available at fabric stores) to slow that process.

ZIGZAG STITCH

Using your conventional machine, run a zigzag stitch just along the raw edge. This is a good alternative if you don't have a serger but want your seam allowances to look more professional.

secure stitching
HOLD TO IT

This type of stitching does not form seams. It is used to secure hems or other edge finishing (such as the borders of pockets) and is visible on the garment—unlike seam stitching, which is hidden to the eye.

TOPSTITCHING

This stitch is sewn on the face of the garment parallel to a seam and usually placed ¼" away from the seam—think of the row or two of topstitching down the inseam or your jeans. Topstitching secures the seam even more—you will notice that in places with heavy traffic

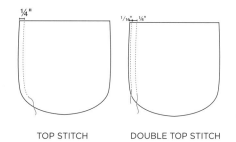

TOP STITCH   DOUBLE TOP STITCH

like the crotch or pocket openings the topstitching will add additional support to the seam. It can also be used for decorative purposes (you can choose contrast or metallic thread, for instance, or use thick thread for a sportier look).

EDGESTITCHING

This stitch is placed only ¹⁄₁₆" or ⅛" (1 or 2mm) away from seam line. Because the stitching is right at the seam, it's meant to not be as noticeable as topstitching; you probably won't want to use decorative thread here.

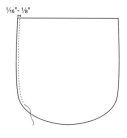

EDGE STITCH

UNDERSTITCHING

This stitch uses edgestitching to sew the seam allowance to another part of the garment, usually a facing (a mirror image piece that goes inside the garment as a method of invisibly concealing the edge; see below for more on these). In this type of situation, understitching is used to secure the facing or other piece from flipping over.

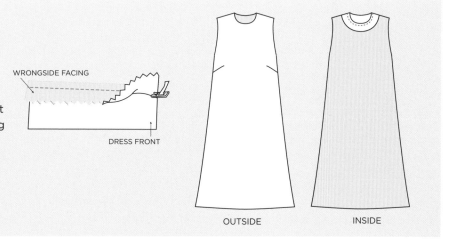

WRONGSIDE FACING

DRESS FRONT

OUTSIDE   INSIDE

living on the edge
FINISHING RAW OPENINGS

When all your seams are sewn, you're still not finished. The final step in sewing is to cover up the raw edges of the garment, such as the hem of the skirt or sleeve, armholes (if there are no sleeves), and necklines. Necklines are usually finished with collars; sleeves are generally finished with cuffs and hems. But some styles don't come with these extra pieces. Sleeveless dresses or dresses with plain necklines are often finished with what's called *facing.* This is a piece of fabric that faces the body on the inside of the garment and forms a mirror image of the shape of the opening. (Have a look inside some of your sleeveless or open-neck dresses, and you'll get the idea.) Another alternative to finishing this type of opening is to line the entire dress. Unlike a facing, which covers just the small area around an opening, a lining extends to cover the entire inside of the garment. You can also do a combination of a facing with a lining attached to the edge of the facing. This requires another seam to sew, but it's often much nicer looking than a simple facing because it conceals the facing's edge automatically.

You can also finish these openings with bias binding, a strip of bias-cut fabric (that is, cut on a 45-degree angle) that wraps around the raw edge and is topstitched or edgestitched to the body. The bottom of a garment is almost always finished with a hem. You can also finish edges using trims. Read on for more about each of these options, and how to sew them.

FACINGS: THE FACTS

Generally, facing is made of the same fabric as the garment. (It's a good idea to apply interfacing—a stabilizing iron-on webbed fabric—to the wrong side of the facing to keep it from flipping around, wrinkling, and bunching). Here's how to sew it on:

1. Trace a 2" (5cm) wide facing around the front and back necklines of your pattern pieces.

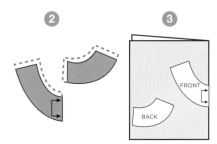
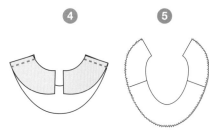

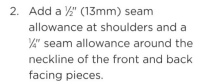

2. Add a ½" (13mm) seam allowance at shoulders and a ¼" seam allowance around the neckline of the front and back facing pieces.

3. Fold fabric in half. Place front facing piece on the fold. Place the back facing piece on fabric. Cut out.

4. With the right sides together, sew front facing to back facing at the shoulders.

5. Finish the raw edge of the facing with a serger, pinking shears, or zigzag stitch (that's the edge that is *not* being joined to the body of the garment).

6. Pin the facing to the garment, right sides together.

7. Stitch the two pieces together, leaving a ¼" (6mm) seam allowance. Clip or notch the seam allowances where it's necessary along any curved seams.

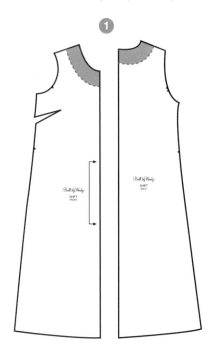

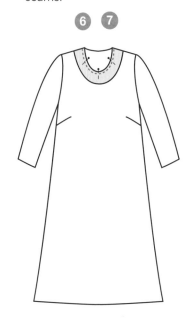

8. Press the resulting seam allowance toward the facing.

9. Understitch. Run an edgestitch along the top of the seam allowance near the facing edge, thus securing the seam allowance to the facing side and eliminating bulk.

10. To prevent the facing from flipping out, you'll also need to secure it inside the garment. You can do this by hand-stitching the facing to the shoulder seam or side seam. Or you can use your machine's blind-hem stitch to secure the entire facing to the body. (This is a bit time consuming, but it looks nice and clean.)

TIP:

Some designs call for a facing to be sewn with its right side to the wrong side of the *garment*, so that when it flips around, the facing is on the *outside* of the garment as a decorative element. It then gets topstitched down to the garment—you can even insert some piping first!

8 **9**

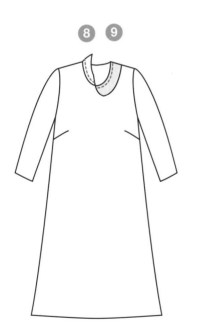

10

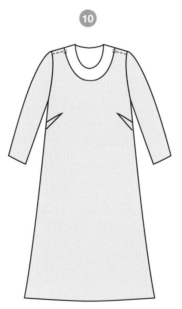

WORLD OF INTERIORS: LININGS

It's always best to line dresses fully when they're sheer or made from a scratchy or heavy fabric. If you're making a lightweight cotton batiste dress, for instance, lining it will prevent it from being see-through and add bulk to make it feel a bit more luxurious and substantial. Sometimes, finishing edges with only a facing can look cheap, especially when the facing shows through a sheer dress. Also, in the fall and winter, when you're probably going to be wearing tights or hose with your dresses, lining keeps the main fabric from sticking to your legs and bunching up. A lining is basically like a built-in slip, whether it's protecting you from itchy and clingy fabrics or protecting your modesty.

BOUND FOR GLORY: BIAS BINDING

Bias binding (also known as bias tape) is a strip of fabric that wraps around a raw edge to finish it. You can buy basic solid colors at the store, but it's more fun to make your own if you feel like getting creative.

Store-bought binding comes with its edges already folded over, so simply slip your garment's raw edge inside the folds of the binding and edgestitch it. Start and finish at a seam—that way, the seam joining the ends of the binding will be less conspicuous.

Homemade binding is made using a bias tape maker (one of my all-time favorite inventions) or by carefully measuring and cutting a 1"- (2.5cm-) wide strip of fabric along the bias. If you measure and cut your own:

1. Prepare it by pressing the strip in half.

2. Fold under the raw edges along the length of the binding.

3. Insert the raw edge of the garment into the folded piece, and edgestitch the binding down.

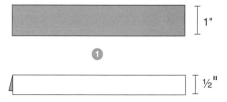

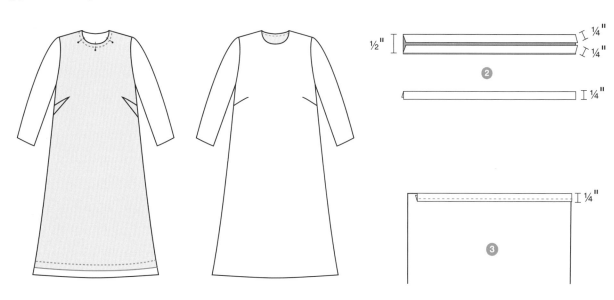

HEMMING AND HAWING: HEMS

The thickness of a garment's hem depends on several factors: the shape of the hem, the fabric type, and how you want it to look. No matter what type of hem you're sewing, one thing is crucial: You must measure and press it carefully. Keep your clear ruler at hand, and make use of it. Check and recheck to make sure the line isn't sloping at an angle, and try the garment on before you sew the hem.

Topstitched Hem

Just fold back the hem and stitch it down with the stitch line showing on the outside of the dress. This is the classic hem used in sportswear. It's not the dressiest, but it will work just fine for most projects.

Blindstitch Hem

This hem looks just like it sounds, which is to say it doesn't look like anything: Only one out of every few stitches pricks the outer surface, so no stitching lines are visible. It makes for a cleaner, more professional look, especially if you're working with silk

or other extra-fine fabrics. That said, I don't recommend it for most home sewers; it can get easily messed up, and the folding process is tricky. Some machines come with a blind-hem foot, or you can buy one and attach it yourself (just make sure that your machine is able to do zigzag stitches; such machines will usually do a blind-hem stitch, too).

Hem finishing

As with all edges and seams, you must finish hems. When hemming, you can do a "clean finish," which means you fold up the hem twice, thus hiding the fabric edge inside the hem. This generally looks nicer than just folding the hem once and is

a must if the inside of the hem might be visible, such as for a wide skirt or sleeve that might reveal its interior as you move. The easiest hem is just a basic hem where you finish the raw edge with a standard finish such as serging, pinking, or zigzag stitching.

To make a clean finish hem with a 1½" (3.8 cm) hem allowance:

1. Fold back the raw edge ¼" (6mm).

2. Fold it up again 1" (2.5cm).

3. Press, pin, and topstitch the hem ⅞" (2.2cm).

To make a basic hem with a 1½" (3.8cm) hem allowance:

1. Finish the raw edge of the fabric with your choice of finish.

2. Fold back edge 1½" (3.8cm)

3. Press, pin, and topstitch the hem.

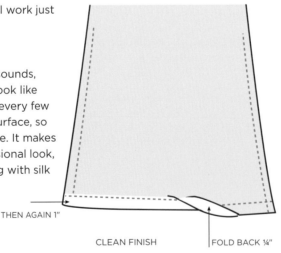

THEN AGAIN 1"

CLEAN FINISH   FOLD BACK ¼"

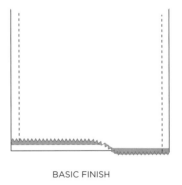

BASIC FINISH

the heat is on
PRESSING

TUNE IT UP: TRIMS

A quick, easy, and fun way to finish a hem is to stitch some lace trim or rickrack to the raw edge. The most polished-looking way to do this is to place the trim against the raw edge, right sides together, and stitch. Think of it as the same way you would attach a facing, but instead of folding the trim inside and understitching it, you'll flip the trim up, folding the seam inside the neckline or hem. You can then topstitch around the opening to secure the seam to the body.

You must, must, *must* press each seam open after you sew it. Why? Once a seam is joined to another seam, its fate is sealed. If you don't press it first to fully flatten it out, you won't be able to do so correctly after it's joined, and it may create bunching or asymmetry in the garment. Some pieces, such as collars, must be pressed first too, because you'll need to topstitch them before you attach them to the garment's body. Here's how to meet the press.

- Always use a press cloth to protect the fabric from getting damaged by the heat, unless you're working with linen or cotton (which are not so heat sensitive).

- Always press on the wrong side of the fabric. Heat can alter the surface of the fabric, causing it to shine or fade.

- Iron in the direction of the warp (the strongest grain) so that the fabric doesn't stretch out. Be gentle.

- To avoid steam circles from the iron, use a nonsteam iron and spray water directly onto the fabric.

- Place a piece of fabric under the garment so the heat is conducted better.

- Use a piece of fabric to cover small pieces with stitching, such as cuffs, collars, and plackets, to avoid smashing the seams.

an open-and-shut case

BUTTONS AND BUTTONHOLES

Buttons are available in an endless array of colors, shapes, and sizes—and even come without visible holes (a type known as shank buttons)—but they all go on essentially the same way. Don't skip this section, even if you think you know how to do it: If you sew them on right, they'll stay on a lot longer.

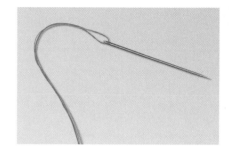

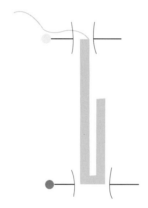

BUTTONHOLES

Hopefully, your machine has an automatic buttonholer; most modern versions do. Set the length that corresponds to your button size—the hole should be ⅛" (3mm) longer than the button width. Make sure that the placket where you're making holes has interfacing attached to make the fabric sturdier—otherwise, your holes might look rumpled and puckered. If you're going to be varying the button layout at all,

measure extremely carefully. Mark the locations first using your clear ruler, making sure the buttonholes are at even intervals and centered perfectly. Start with the bottom button first—mistakes won't be as obvious there. Place the needle *at the top of where the opening will be*, and the machine will *work its way down*. Then fold the fabric and gently snip the hole, finish with sealant or even clear nail polish, and voilà!

THREADING NEEDLES TO SEW BUTTONS

I hate hand-stitching, but it's the only way to attach buttons. Luckily, it's a pretty simple process. To save yourself the hassle of having to stitch through the buttonholes several times, it's easiest to double-thread your needle, creating a thicker thread.

- Cut a length of thread. If you're not sure how much you need, try about 18" (45cm).

- Fold the thread in half and thread the folded tip through the eye of the needle (you might want to use a larger-eyed needle and a threader for help).

- Knot the loose ends (there will be two) together. I like to knot them at least twice to make sure that the knot is big enough.

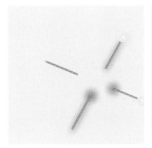  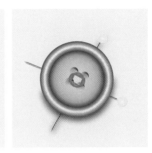

ATTACHING BUTTONS

Keep in mind that if a button is sewn on too tightly, it won't have any wiggle room. You need to give it some space by creating a shank—basically, a stem of wrapped thread—so the button can move around without snapping off easily. Starting from underneath the placket, pierce the surface. Make a couple of stitches to secure the thread in place.

Place a pin or pins where the button will lie to create some space between the button and the garment. Then place the button, and tie the thread through the holes at least three or four times. Remove the pin. Underneath the button, wind the thread around the thread holding the button on a few times. This will create a shank for added strength and flexibility.

Bring the thread through to the wrong side of fabric. Stitch a couple of times to secure it, then knot the loose threads and clip them off.

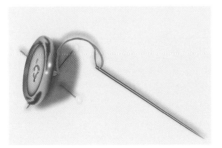 

zip, zip, hooray
SEWING ZIPPERS

There are two common ways to place a zipper: centered (in which the zipper has equal amounts of fabric on each side) and lapped (in which the seam allowance on one side creates a flap to hide the zipper). To keep things streamlined, I will focus on the centered zipper technique; it's much easier and is a good way for beginners to learn. Plus, visible zippers can be a very cool design element—you can even pick a plastic one in a contrasting color, or go with bold, chunky metal. The patterns in this book can use a regular 22" (56cm) zipper (available in many colors) or an invisible zipper, a very thin zipper that is designed to be nearly invisible from the outside of the garment. These look much fancier, but they require a special invisible zipper foot that you'll have to buy. If you're a beginner, do yourself a favor and start with regular zippers first.

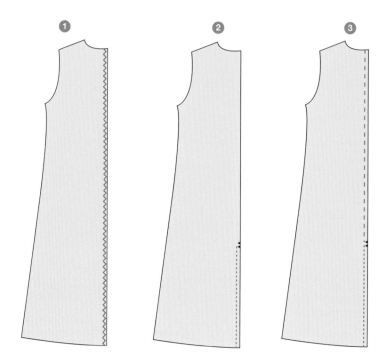

Centered zipper application:

1. Finish the seams allowances along the center back seam of the dress.

2. With the right sides together, sew the center back seam up from the hem to the notch point as marked on the pattern. The notch indicates where the zipper will end.

3. Change your machine's stitch length to the longest setting, and machine-baste the seam from the notch to the neck.

4. Press the seam allowance open. Place the closed zipper face down onto the pressed-open seam allowance with zipper pull about ½" (13mm) below the neck edge.

5. Tape the zipper to the seam using regular clear tape or special basting tape.

6. Turn garment over to right side and trace a line using your marking pen, chalk, or tailor's wax to mark a

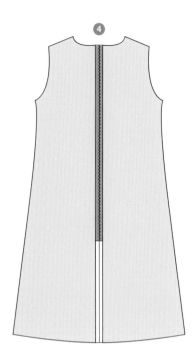

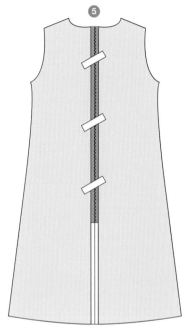

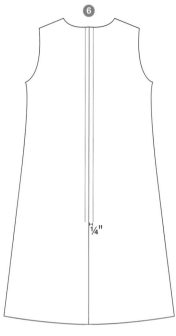

line ¼" (6mm) away from the center back seam on each side from the bottom of the zipper to the top neck edge.

7. Using the zipper foot on your machine, topstitch along your line from bottom of zipper to the top neck edge. Do this on each side.

8. Stitch a horizontal line beneath the end stopper to connect the stitching line on each side. Be careful not to hit the end stopper, or you'll break your needle.

pockets
THE INSIDE STORY

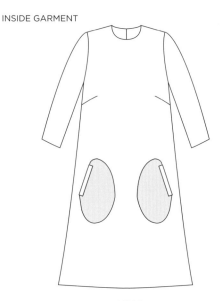 INSIDE GARMENT

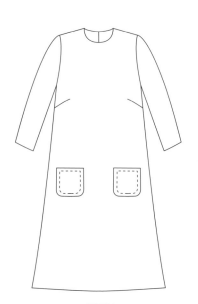

PATCH

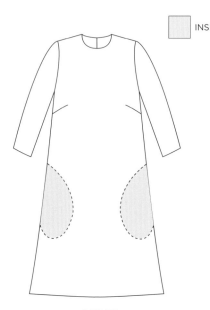

INSEAM

WELT

The great thing about pockets is that they can serve a function or add a cute design element—or both! There are three types of pockets: patch, in-seam, and welt. The choice between the types depends on the fit and design of the garment. A patch pocket is attached on top of the garment and is functional for tight garments where it would be difficult to put your hand inside of the garment; jeans are a great example. You can make these pockets any size or shape, with or without a flap, making them a great place to play with design. An inseam pocket opens along the seam and is great for a roomier garment, such as a loose dress or trousers that leave room to fit your hands inside. It's also great if you want the function of a pocket but don't want it showing on the outside of your dress. It creates a more sophisticated look, as opposed to the sportier look of a patch pocket. The only limitation is that you need to put the pocket where there is a seam on the garment. The welt pocket is sort of a combination of a patch and an inseam pocket. The welt shows up on the garment as a slit; thus, it's not hidden like the inseam pocket, but it is more sophisticated than the patch. The welt pocket can be inserted anywhere on the garment and is not limited to a seam (think the back of dress trousers). Since the pocket is actually inside of the garment, you do need consider whether there's room for the pocket to lie inside the garment. Welt pockets are pretty difficult to sew—probably too advanced for this book, which is why I won't go into detail about how to sew them.

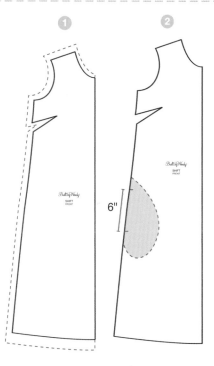

Sewing a patch pocket:

1. Finish the top edge of pocket with your choice of finish: serging, pinking, or zigzag stitching.

2. Fold back the top edge 1" (2.5cm), leaving the right sides together, and stitch with a ½" (13mm) seam allowance down from the top edge along the sides of the folded top.

3. Flip the top edge over, sandwiching the seam allowances inside the fold. Iron the seam allowances inside.

4. Flip the pocket over and topstitch a line ¾" (2cm) below the top edge.

5. Place the pocket onto the right side of the garment, then topstitch the sides of the pockets to the garment.

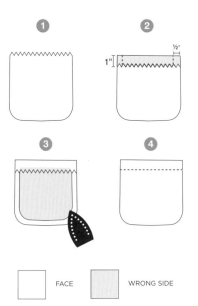

Making an inseam pocket:

1. Add seam allowances to your pattern pieces.

2. Mark 2 notches 6" (15cm) apart on the side seam in the place where you want your pocket. Trace the shape of a pocket similar to the illustration. An easy trick is to place your hand on the area through the notches and then trace around your hand. This helps ensure that the pocket is deep enough. Start the pocket 1" (2.5cm) above and below the notches.

3. Trace this pocket shape and transfer to a new piece of paper. Add ½″ (13mm) seam allowances around the curved pocket.

4. Once you cut out your garment, place the pockets' wrong sides to right side of the garment front. Stitch together between the notches.

5. Turn the pocket inside of the garment, straightening out the side seam allowances.

6. Lay the back pocket on top of the front pocket, wrong sides together, and stitch around the curved edge.

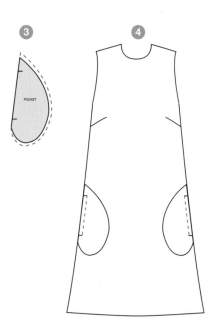

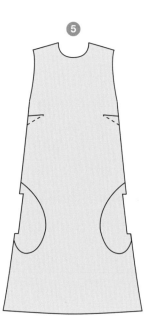

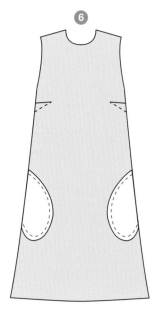

7. Flip the garment over, flatten out the pockets and straighten out the side seams to neaten the opening.

8. With right sides together, stitch front to back body pieces together at the side seams. Be careful not to catch the front pocket opening in the seam allowance. A nice trick is to use a zipper foot along that part so that you get close to the pocket opening's edge.

9. Open the garment flat, right side up, and you will see a nice pocket hidden inside the seam!

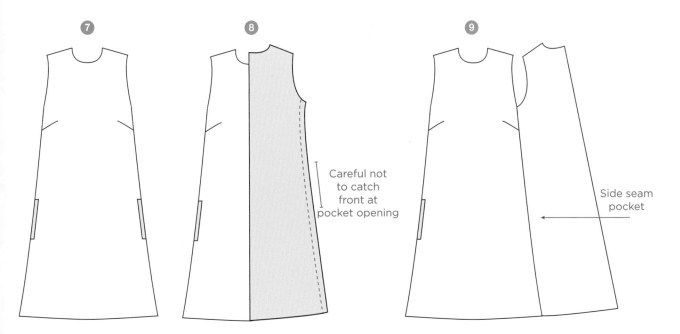

Careful not to catch front at pocket opening

Side seam pocket

CHAPTER 5

THE SHEATH DRESS

THIS SIMPLE, STREAMLINED SILHOUETTE IS INCREDIBLY VERSATILE and flattering for all shapes and sizes, thanks to its built-in waist definition and easy-to-play-with raglan sleeves. The basic pattern has cap sleeves and a fitted shape created by *front* darts, and it's knee length—but as you'll see, changing that can result in a totally different look. Whether you're making a dress for business or pleasure, this chapter has something fresh to offer.

workin' nine to five

As its name implies, this is a great dress to wear to the office. It has a polished, professional feel and keeps you covered, but still exudes a structured, slightly sixties-inspired chic. I'm suggesting making it in bright, cheery orange linen for spring, but you can also whip it up in a nice wool crepe for fall. It pairs equally well with flats, heels, and boots. Show 'em who's boss!

supplies

2 yards (1.8m) orange linen
½ yard (46cm) fusible interfacing
22" (56cm) orange invisible zipper
5 orange 24 line buttons

pattern adjustments

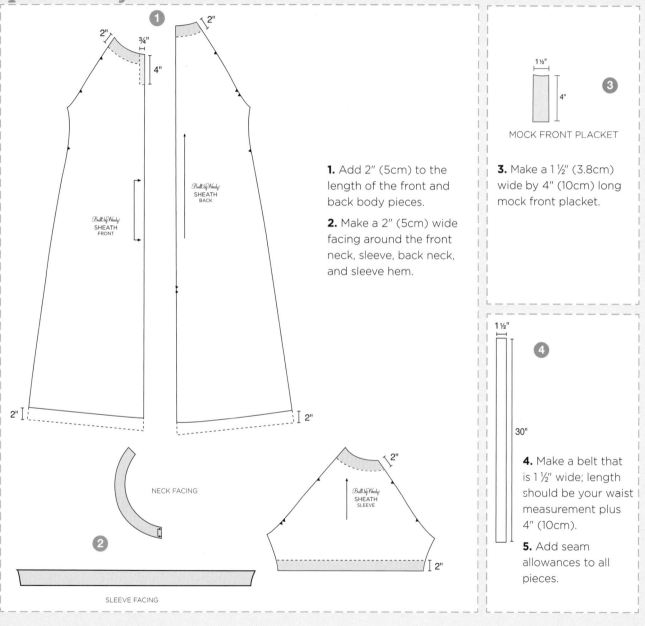

1. Add 2″ (5cm) to the length of the front and back body pieces.

2. Make a 2″ (5cm) wide facing around the front neck, sleeve, back neck, and sleeve hem.

3. Make a 1 ½″ (3.8cm) wide by 4″ (10cm) long mock front placket.

4. Make a belt that is 1 ½″ wide; length should be your waist measurement plus 4″ (10cm).

5. Add seam allowances to all pieces.

MOCK FRONT PLACKET

NECK FACING

SLEEVE FACING

cutting

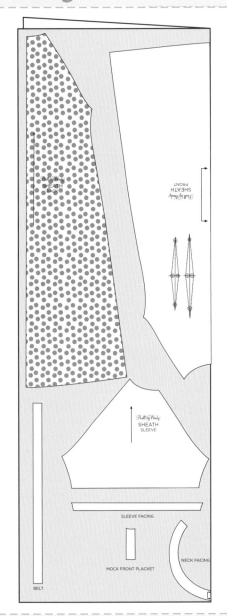

Self: 44" (112cm)

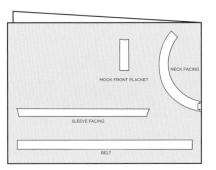

Fusible interfacing: 44" (112cm)

G.I. Jane

By simply changing the fabric and tweaking the details, you can create a totally different look using basically the same pattern: Just check out this army-style minidress! Make the dress in olive green twill, and add some military-inspired details like cargo pockets and epaulettes. Instead of a making a belt, topstitch a tunnel around the waist and insert a drawstring. Shorten the basic pattern about 3"–4" (7.5–10cm) to achieve a minidress length.

sewing

1. Iron fusible interfacing to the wrong side of the mock front placket, sleeve and neck facings, and belt.

2. Sew the front darts.

3. Fold back the mock front placket's seam allowances, pin it to the center front body, and edgestitch it down.

4. With right sides together, sew the center back seam from the hem to the zipper notch. Baste it from the notch to the neck.

5. Press the center back seam open and insert the zipper.

6. With right sides together, sew the front sleeve to the front arm-hole.

7. With right sides together, sew the back sleeve to the back arm-hole.

8. With right side of the sleeve's facing to the wrong side of the sleeve body, sew the facing hem to the sleeve hem.

sewing

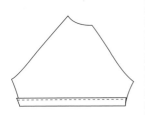

9. Turn the sleeve facing to the right side of the sleeve, fold back the raw edge, and edgestitch the facing to the sleeve.

10. With right sides together, sew the front body to the back body at side seams from the hem up to the sleeve hem.

11. With right sides together, sew the neck facing to the neckline.

12. Press the seam towards the neck facing, understitch the seam, and tack it to the center back zipper tape.

13. Fold back the hem 2″ (5cm) and topstitch.

14. With right sides together, sew the belt pieces together, leaving a 3″ (7.5cm) opening.

15. Turn the belt inside out, press it, and topstitch. Fit the belt around the waist and mark the locations for the two buttons and buttonholes.

16. Attach the buttons and sew the buttonholes.

capri sundress

The billowing shape of this classic sundress makes this a personal favorite of mine for wearing on vacation: It's breezy, feminine, and perfect for those moments when you need something sweet and easy to throw on and go. The bold colors of this print make it a bit glamorous in that boating-on-the-Amalfi Coast sort of way.

supplies

1¾ yards (1.6m) lightweight floral cotton

pattern adjustments

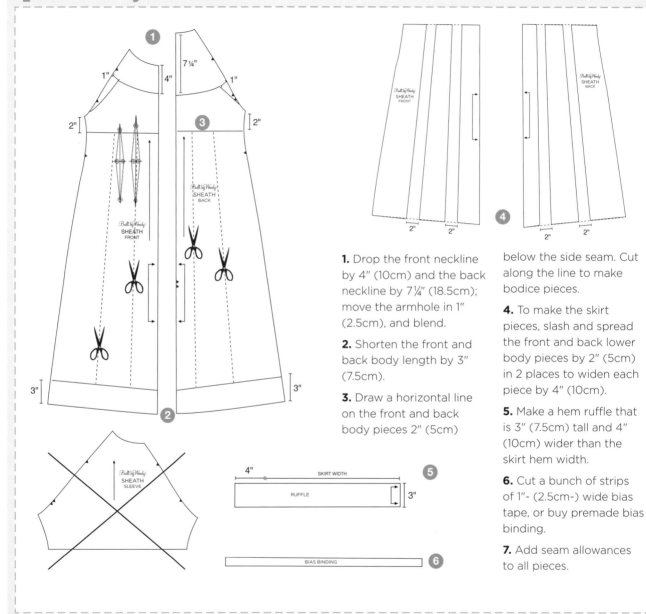

1. Drop the front neckline by 4″ (10cm) and the back neckline by 7¼″ (18.5cm); move the armhole in 1″ (2.5cm), and blend.

2. Shorten the front and back body length by 3″ (7.5cm).

3. Draw a horizontal line on the front and back body pieces 2″ (5cm)

below the side seam. Cut along the line to make bodice pieces.

4. To make the skirt pieces, slash and spread the front and back lower body pieces by 2″ (5cm) in 2 places to widen each piece by 4″ (10cm).

5. Make a hem ruffle that is 3″ (7.5cm) tall and 4″ (10cm) wider than the skirt hem width.

6. Cut a bunch of strips of 1″- (2.5cm-) wide bias tape, or buy premade bias binding.

7. Add seam allowances to all pieces.

cutting

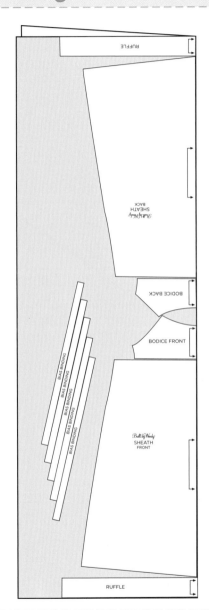

RUFFLE

SHEATH
BACK
Built By Wendy

BODICE BACK

BODICE FRONT

BIAS BINDING
BIAS BINDING
BIAS BINDING
BIAS BINDING
BIAS BINDING
BIAS BINDING

SHEATH
FRONT
Built By Wendy

RUFFLE

Self: 44" (112cm)

La Boheme

Every glamorous *donna* needs something special to wear after dark. And with this same pattern, you can create a totally different look—one that's dressy enough for the opera! Just buy some black velvet, add to the pattern's length to make a floor-length hem, and use a decorative binding around the neckline, making sure to measure carefully since you won't want sundress-style adjustable ties.

sewing

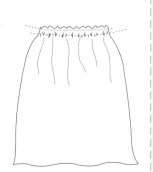

1. Gather the front and back skirts at the top edge.

2. With right sides together, sew the front bodice to the front skirt. Do the same for the back pieces.

3. Gather the front and back ruffles at the top edge. Fold back the hem ½" (13mm), and topstitch.

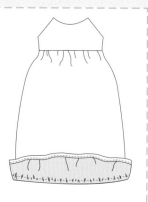

4. With right sides together, sew the front skirt to the front ruffle. Do the same for the back pieces.

5. With right sides together, sew the front body to the back body at the side seams, moving from hems to underarms.

6. Finish the center front and back necklines with bias binding.

7. Leaving 20" (51cm) of binding free on each end, attach the bias binding around each armhole. Continue stitching the binding extensions past the armholes to finish the straps. Fold the ends of the binding inward about ¼" (6mm) and stitch them shut to finish.

8. Tie the ends of the extension straps into bows.

PROJECT 3

cannes do

This is another great shape to wear on vacation; it makes me think of high rolling on the French Riviera as the paparazzi flashbulbs pop. Crisp white silk or cotton keeps it lightweight and fresh, while the neck facing on the outside is the perfect place to really get creative with decorative trim. Bust out the BeDazzler and add a touch of tough chic with some nailheads, or use rhinestones to give the look some serious sparkle. Go ahead—embellish away!

supplies

1¾ yards (1.6m) white cotton or silk
½ yard (50cm) fusible interfacing
22" (56cm) white zipper
Various rhinestones and nailheads

pattern adjustments

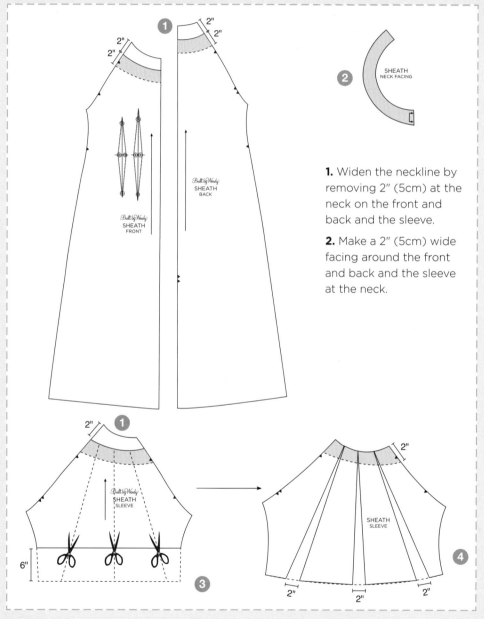

1. Widen the neckline by removing 2″ (5cm) at the neck on the front and back and the sleeve.

2. Make a 2″ (5cm) wide facing around the front and back and the sleeve at the neck.

3. Add 6″ (15cm) to the sleeve length.

4. Slash and spread the sleeve piece by about 2″ (5cm) in 3 places to make it about 6″ (15cm) wider at the bottom, keeping the armhole width close to the original width.

5. Add seam allowances to all pieces.

cutting

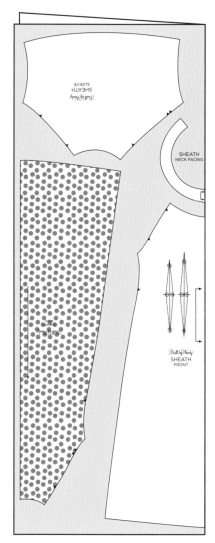

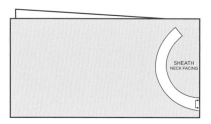

Fusible interfacing: 44″ (112cm) wide

Self: 44″ (112cm) wide

Urban Peasant

To create a totally different look using this project's pattern, try using black cotton, inserting a ruffle into the neck facing, and making a ruffle hem for a chic, modern take on the classic peasant sundress. This design would also look cute in a floral pattern.

sewing

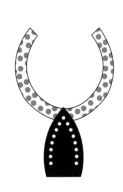

1. Iron the fusible interfacing to the wrong side of the neck facing.

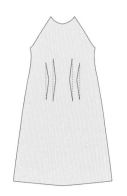

2. Sew the front darts.

3. With right sides together, sew the front sleeves to the front armholes.

4. With right sides together, sew the back sleeves to the back armholes.

5. With right sides together, sew the center back seam from the hem up to the zipper notch and baste it from the notch to the neck.

6. Press the center back seam open and insert the zipper.

7. With right side of the neck facing to the wrong side of the dress neckline, sew the facing to the neckline.

8. Press the seam toward the body, understitch, and turn the facing onto the body face.

9. Fold back the facing's raw edge, press, and edgestitch the facing to the body.

10. With right sides together, sew the front body to the back body at the side seams from the skirt hem up to the sleeve hem.

11. Fold back the skirt hem 2″ (5cm) and topstitch.

12. Make a ¼″ (6mm) clean-finish sleeve hem.

13. Decorate the neck facing however you like; try gluing rhinestones and applying nailheads.

drawstring dress

This easy-to-make, easy-to-throw-on lilac cotton dress is the ultimate summer basic. Its drawstring waist and airy fabric make it ideal for hot weather, while the pockets add a funky, functional twist. You can also try making it without pockets for a very simple piece that will highlight your favorite jewelry beautifully. You'll love it so much, you'll want to make it in every color!

supplies

1½ yards (1.4m) lilac cotton

¼ yard (23cm) fusible interfacing

1 yard (91cm) ¾" (2cm) wide lilac cotton twill tape

2 yards (1.8m) lilac cotton cord

Four 24 line buttons

1 yard (91cm) bias binding

pattern adjustments

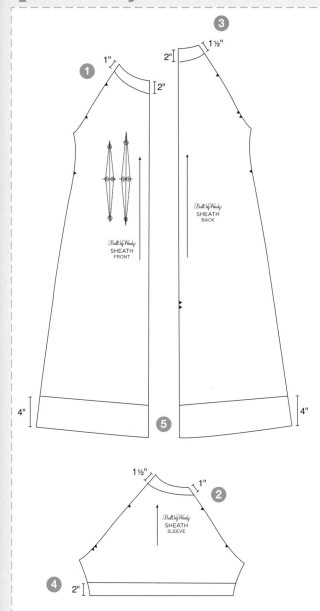

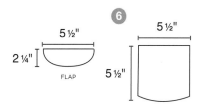

1. Drop the front neckline by 2″ (5cm) at the center front and 1″ (2.5cm) at the shoulder, and blend.

2. Drop the sleeve neckline by 1″ (2.5cm) at the front and 1½″ (3.8cm) at back, and blend.

3. Drop the back neckline by 2″ (5cm) at the center back and 1½″ (3.8cm) at the shoulder, and blend.

4. Shorten the sleeves by 2″ (5cm) at the bottom.

5. Shorten the front and back body length by 4″ (10cm) at the bottom.

6. Make two skirt patch pockets that measure 5½″ by 5½″ (14cm x 14cm) and flaps that measure 2¼″ by 5½″ (5.5cm x 14cm). Round the bottom corners.

7. Make a front bodice flap detail measuring 4″ by 2″ (10cm x 5cm). Round the bottom corners.

8. Add seam allowances to all pieces.

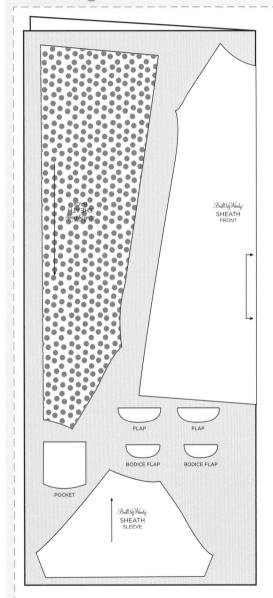

Self: 44" (112cm) wide

Fusible interfacing: 44"
(112cm) wide

Rainbow Brights

Try making each
component in a
different color of
cotton (a technique
called *color-blocking*)
for a fun, summery
way to reinvent this
project that's lot less
complicated than it
looks. Bold sherbet
hues will keep all eyes
on you!

sewing

1. Iron fusible interfacing to the wrong sides of the pocket flaps.

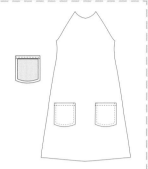

2. Fold back all pocket seam allowances, topstitch the top edges, pin them to the front body, and topstitch them down.

3. With right sides together, sew each pair of pocket flap pieces around the sides and the bottom edge. Turn each flap right side out, press, and topstitch around the edge.

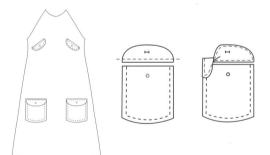

4. Fold back each pocket flap's top raw edge and topstitch ½" (13mm) above the pocket. Make button-holes and attach the buttons.

5. With right sides together, sew the bodice flaps around the sides and the bottom edges. Turn them right sides out, press, and topstitch around the edges.

6. Fold back the top edge of each bodice flap and topstitch it to the bodice. Secure the flap to the body with a button stitched through the flap and the body.

7. With right sides together, sew the front sleeves to the front armholes.

sewing

8. With right sides together, sew the back sleeves to the back armholes.

9. Fold back the sleeve hems 1″ (2.5cm) and topstitch.

10. With right sides together, sew the front body to the back body along the side seams.

11. Finish the neckline with bias binding.

12. With right sides together, sew the back pieces together.

13. Pin ¾″ (2cm) wide cotton tape around the waist to create a drawstring tunnel and edgestitch it to the body. Leave a 2″ (5cm) opening at the center front. Insert cord for a drawstring.

14. Fold back the hem 1½″ (3.8cm) and topstitch.

PROJECT 5

overall improvement

This classic jumper is a feminine update on old-school workwear. Whether the look you're after is girly artist or handy carpenter, it's the perfect layering piece for a cool, fuss-free vibe. Contrast topstitching adds visual interest and a sturdy feel.

supplies

1¼ yards (1.1m) denim

pattern adjustments

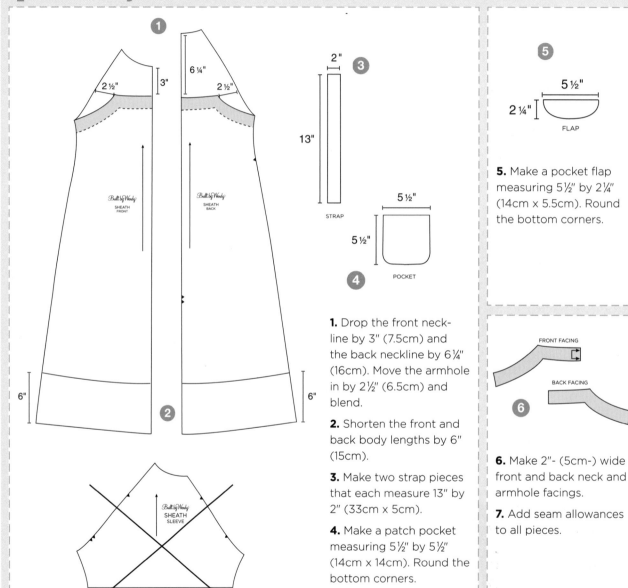

1. Drop the front neckline by 3″ (7.5cm) and the back neckline by 6¼″ (16cm). Move the armhole in by 2½″ (6.5cm) and blend.

2. Shorten the front and back body lengths by 6″ (15cm).

3. Make two strap pieces that each measure 13″ by 2″ (33cm x 5cm).

4. Make a patch pocket measuring 5½″ by 5½″ (14cm x 14cm). Round the bottom corners.

5. Make a pocket flap measuring 5½″ by 2¼″ (14cm x 5.5cm). Round the bottom corners.

6. Make 2″- (5cm-) wide front and back neck and armhole facings.

7. Add seam allowances to all pieces.

cutting

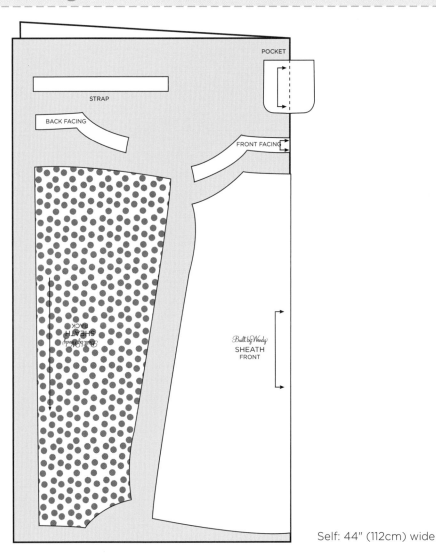

POCKET

STRAP

BACK FACING

FRONT FACING

Built by Wendy
SHEATH
BACK

Built by Wendy
SHEATH
FRONT

Self: 44" (112cm) wide

Too Cool for School

Try making the same pattern with a Peter Pan collar and contrast banded hem for a chic schoolgirl effect. In black wool crepe with a white organdy collar, it will look more Parisian ingenue than kindergartener!

sewing

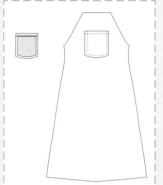 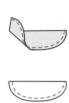

1. Fold back all pocket seam allowances, topstitch the top edge, pin the pocket to the front body, and topstitch.

2. With right sides together, sew the pocket flap around the sides and bottom edge. Turn the right side out, press, and topstitch around the edge.

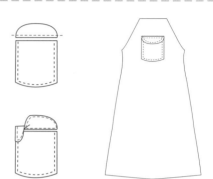

3. Fold back the pocket flap's top raw edge, and topstitch ½" (13mm) above the pocket.

4. Fold the straps in half lengthwise, sew along the raw edges, turn, press, and topstitch around the edges.

5. With right sides together, sew the back pieces together.

6. With right sides together, sew the back body to the front body along the side seams.

7. Pin the straps to the front and back necks.

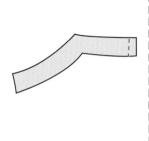

8. With right sides together, sew the back facings together.

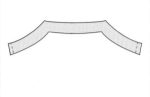

9. With right sides together, sew the back facing to the front facing along the side seams.

10. With right sides together, sew the facing to the body around the neckline and armholes, making sure to catch the strap ends in the stitching. Understitch and tack the facing to the side seams.

11. Fold back the hem 1″ and topstitch.

bow wow

Shown here in a pretty peach silk linen, this dress is perfect for a Sunday brunch with your boyfriend's folks. It's demure, yet the unique sleeve-seam slits let you show an unexpected flash of skin. You can also try making it in wool tweed with shiny faux-leather binding for a fall-friendly look (just add tights and boots).

supplies

1¾ yard (1.6m) peach silk linen
22″ (56cm) peach zipper

pattern adjustments

1. Drop the front neckline by 2″ (5cm) at the center front and blend to the shoulder.

2. Move the front armhole seam in ½″ (13mm) and blend down by 4″ (10cm).

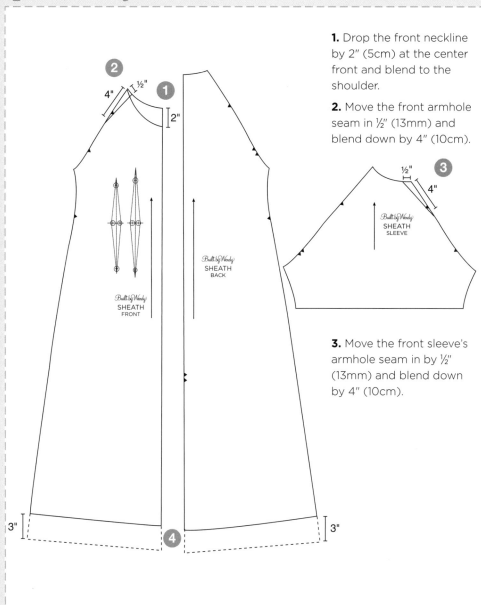

3. Move the front sleeve's armhole seam in by ½″ (13mm) and blend down by 4″ (10cm).

4. Add 3″ (7.5cm) to the front and back body length at the bottom.

5. Add seam allowances to all pieces.

6. Make a 1½″ (3.8cm) wide strip for bias binding. The length should be about 20″ (51cm) or whatever can fit onto the fabric.

cutting

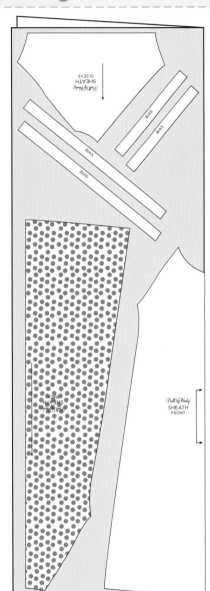

Self: 44" (112cm) wide

Mod World

For a new twist on this pattern, try shortening the dress's length about 6" (15cm) for a sassy mini length. Use contrasting colors (such as black and white) for the body and sleeves for a graphic Op Art look.

sewing

1. With right sides together, sew the back pieces together from the hem to the center back notch. Baste from the notch to the neckline.

2. Press the center back seam open and insert the zipper.

3. With right sides together, sew the front sleeves to the front arm-holes from the neckline to the notch.

4. Press the seam open, folding back the arm-hole seam allowances. Topstitch around the opening.

5. With right sides together, sew the back sleeves to the back armholes.

6. With right sides together, sew the front body to the back body at the side seams from the hem up to the sleeve hem.

7. Fold back the bottom hem 1½″ (3.8cm) and sleeve hem 1″ (2.5cm), and topstitch.

8. Finish the center front neckline with bias binding, extending the ties 10″ (25.5cm) past each side slit.

9. Finish the back neckline and the sleeves with bias binding, extending the ties 10″ (25.5cm) past the front of the sleeves.

10. Make a bias binding belt measuring 60″ (152.5cm) and tie it on.

PROJECT 7

baja fresh

This classic pullover is the ultimate beach coverup—perfect for sitting by a bonfire on the beach in the 'Bu. Heavy striped cotton gives it that authentic Baja look, but this girlified version fits far better than anything you might pick up from a south-of-the-border street vendor.

supplies

2½ yards (2.3m) multicolored striped cotton
½ yard (46cm) fusible interfacing
1 yard (91cm) cotton cord

pattern adjustments

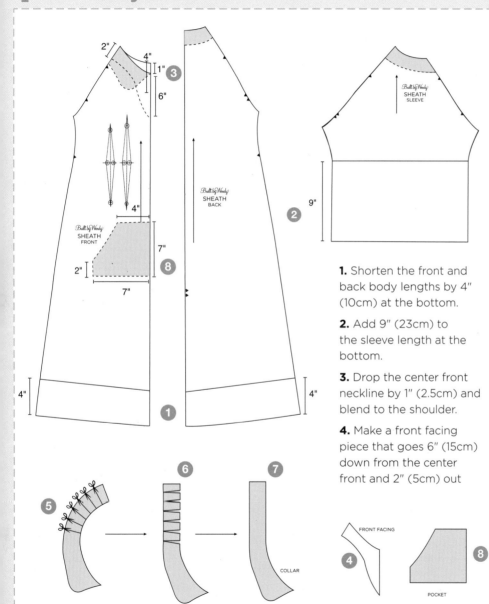

from the shoulder. Blend the shape using a French curve. Make a center front notch for slit placement 4″ (10cm) down from the center front neckline.

5. Make a collar piece that goes 2½″ (6.5cm) out around the back and sleeve necklines. Draw a curve reaching to the center front.

6. Make slash lines on the back of the collar and half of the sleeve areas.

7. Spread the slashed area into a straight line.

8. Make a 7″- (18cm-) high kangaroo pocket with a top edge measuring 4″ (10cm) wide, a bottom edge measuring 7″ (18cm) wide (which will be 14″ [35.5cm] wide when the pocket is cut on the fold), and a 2″ (5cm) long side seam. Draw angled openings from the side seam to the top edge.

9. Add seam allowances to all pieces.

1. Shorten the front and back body lengths by 4″ (10cm) at the bottom.

2. Add 9″ (23cm) to the sleeve length at the bottom.

3. Drop the center front neckline by 1″ (2.5cm) and blend to the shoulder.

4. Make a front facing piece that goes 6″ (15cm) down from the center front and 2″ (5cm) out

cutting

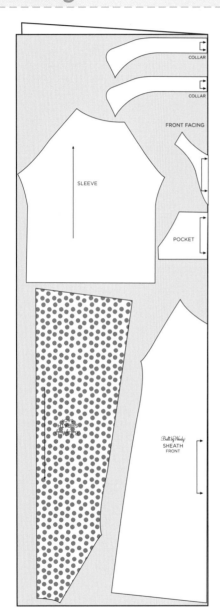

COLLAR

COLLAR

FRONT FACING

SLEEVE

POCKET

Built by Wendy
SHEATH
FRONT

Self: 44″ (112cm) wide

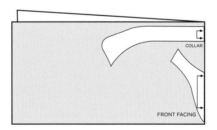

COLLAR

FRONT FACING

Fusible interfacing: 44″ (112cm) wide

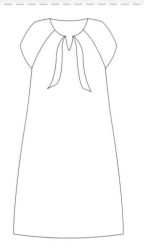

Sea Change

Speaking of easy oceanside dresses, why not try using this pattern to make a full-length, short-sleeved dress in breezy chambray? Instead of using cord, make two wider, flowy ties out of taupe silk. Glamorous yet casually comfy, this is a great dress to throw on for an afternoon spent yacht-spotting on the deck.

sewing

1. Iron fusible interfacing to the wrong side of the undercollars and the front facing.

2. With right sides together, sew the back pieces together.

3. With right sides together, sew the front sleeves to the front armholes.

4. With right sides together, sew the back sleeves to the back armholes.

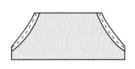

5. Fold back the angled opening on the pocket and topstitch ½" (13mm).

6. Fold back and topstitch the pocket to the front body along the bottom, top, and side edges, leaving the angled edge open.

7. With right sides together, sew the front body to the back body at the side seams from the hem to the sleeve hem.

8. Fold back the hem and the sleeve hem 1" (2.5cm), and topstitch.

sewing

9. With right sides together, sew collar pieces together at center back seam.

10. With right sides together, sew the collar pieces together around the outer edge. Turn them right side out, press, and topstitch.

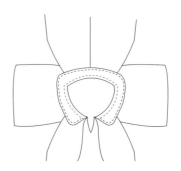

11. With right sides together, sew the collar to the body around the neckline.

12. Tack 15″ (38cm) of cord to each side of the center front neckline at the top of the center slit.

13. With right sides together, sew the front facing to the body's front neckline, on top of the collar.

14. Turn right side out and topstitch around the opening.

oktober dress

This German-inspired dress, made in lilac wool herringbone with a floral-trimmed lace-up front, is a sweetly romantic fall piece that belongs in the closet of every fashionable *frau*. The cotton eyelet underskirt peeking out from beneath softens the wooly menswear fabric. You might also try substituting a solid-color trim on the front and tacking on toggles instead of using the lace-up closure. Why not try it both ways?

supplies

2 yards (1.8m) lightweight lilac-and-white wool herringbone

1¾ yard (1.6m) white cotton eyelet fabric

¼ yard (23cm) floral trim

2 yards (1.8m) black cord

1 pack black store-bought bias binding

6 eyelets

pattern adjustments

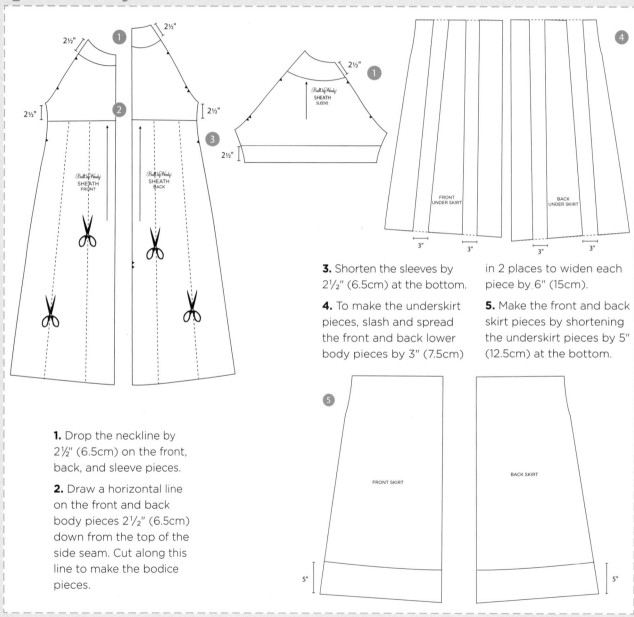

3. Shorten the sleeves by 2½″ (6.5cm) at the bottom.

4. To make the underskirt pieces, slash and spread the front and back lower body pieces by 3″ (7.5cm) in 2 places to widen each piece by 6″ (15cm).

5. Make the front and back skirt pieces by shortening the underskirt pieces by 5″ (12.5cm) at the bottom.

1. Drop the neckline by 2½″ (6.5cm) on the front, back, and sleeve pieces.

2. Draw a horizontal line on the front and back body pieces 2½″ (6.5cm) down from the top of the side seam. Cut along this line to make the bodice pieces.

cutting

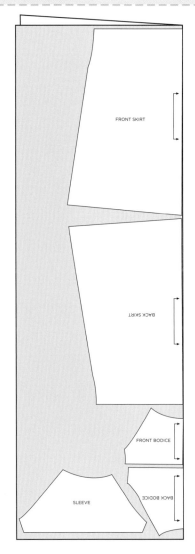

Self: 44" (112cm) wide

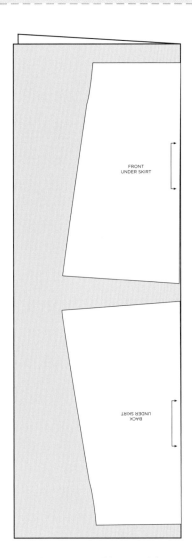

Lining: 44" (112cm) wide

Ballerina Girl

This pattern can look totally different in a solid color without all the trimmings. Try making it in pale pink silk for a simple, graceful dancer-style dress.

sewing

1. Fold back the center front bodice 1" (2.5cm) and edgestitch the floral trim along the folded center front edge.

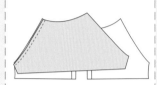

2. With right sides together, sew the front sleeves to the front bodice.

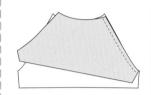

3. With right sides together, sew the back sleeves to the back bodice.

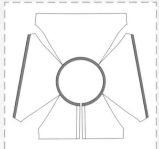

4. Sew the store-bought bias binding around the neckline and sleeve openings.

5. With right sides together, sew the front bodice to the back bodice along the side seams.

6. With right sides together, sew the front skirt piece to the back skirt along the side seams.

7. With right sides together, sew the front underskirt piece to the back underskirt piece along the side seams.

8. Fold back the skirt hem 1½" (3.8cm) and topstitch. Do the same for the underskirt.

9. Insert the underskirt into the skirt, line them up at the side seams, and gather along the top of both skirts at once to form an Empire waist.

10. With right sides together, sew the skirts to the bodice, lining up the pieces at the center and side seam points.

11. Follow the eyelet kit manufacturer's instructions to attach 3 eyelets into the floral trim on each side. Lace the cord through the eyelets, tying the ends of the cord at the neckline, for a lace-up closure.

CHAPTER 6

THE SHIFT DRESS

THE SHIFT IS ONE OF MY GO-TO DRESS PATTERNS FOR A DIFFERENT REASON: ITS STRAIGHT FIT SKIMS OVER THE BODY'S CURVES. This makes for a flatteringly sleek and usually (but not always) more structured silhouette. However, it's not totally stiff; bust darts do give it some shape. The basic pattern included with this book comes with set-in three-quarter-length sleeves, a jewel neckline, and a length that hits just above the knee, but as you'll discover, a few adjustments can transform it into just about any dress you can dream up!

palm beach tunic

The shape of this dress may be ultra-simple, but thanks to the bold floral print, the glam factor is off the charts. It's the perfect piece for when you want to throw something on over your bikini and still look pulled-together.

supplies

2 yards (1.8m) floral cotton batiste

1 yard (91cm) solid cotton batiste

1 yard (91cm) fusible interfacing

pattern adjustments

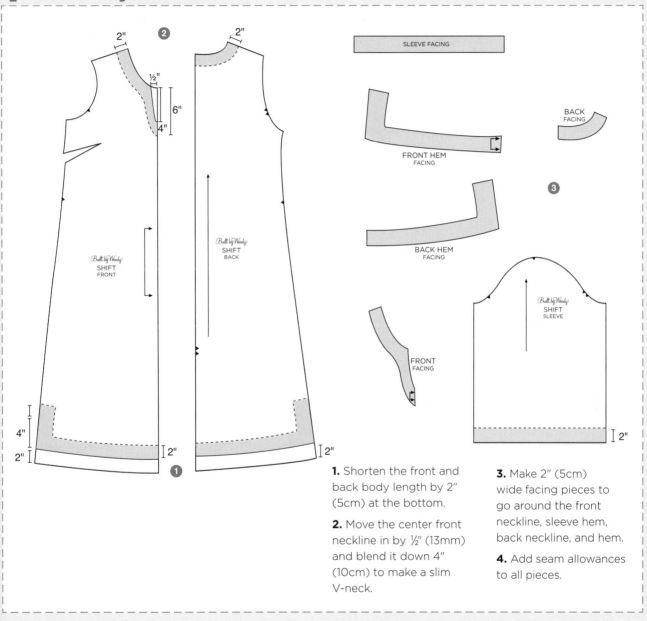

1. Shorten the front and back body length by 2″ (5cm) at the bottom.

2. Move the center front neckline in by ½″ (13mm) and blend it down 4″ (10cm) to make a slim V-neck.

3. Make 2″ (5cm) wide facing pieces to go around the front neckline, sleeve hem, back neckline, and hem.

4. Add seam allowances to all pieces.

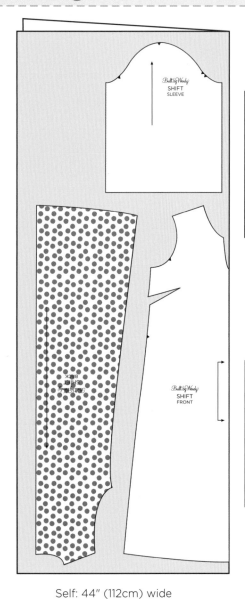

Self: 44" (112cm) wide

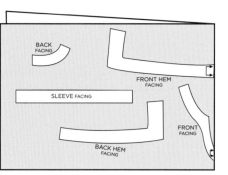

Contrast: 44" (112cm) wide

Fusible interfacing: 44" (112cm) wide

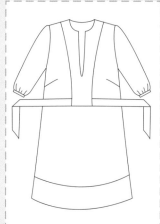

Two-Tone Tunic

For a more sophisticated look (not meant for sand and surf!), try making the facings with a contrasting fabric—I think cream silk facings with a black silk body make an especially elegant combination. Shorten the length about 7" (18cm) for a mini-length piece that looks spectacular with black opaque tights.

sewing

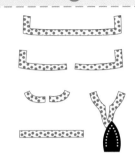

1. Iron fusible interfacing to the wrong side of all facings.

2. Sew the front darts.

3. With right sides together, sew the back pieces together.

4. With right sides together, sew the front body to the back body at the shoulders of the body. Sew the front neck facing to the back neck facing pieces at the "shoulders" as well.

5. With the right side of the neck facing to the wrong side of the body neckline, sew around the neckline.

6. Flip the body right side out, fold back the facing edges, and edgestitch the facing to the body.

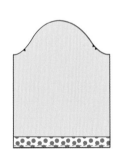

7. With the right side of the sleeve facing to the wrong side of the sleeve, sew along the sleeve hem.

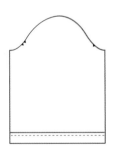

8. Flip the sleeve to its right side, fold back the facing edges, and edgestitch the facing to the sleeve.

sewing

9. With right sides together, sew the sleeve caps to the body armholes.

10. With the right side of the hem facing to the wrong side of the hem, sew around the hem and 4" (10cm) up the side seams.

11. Flip the hem to its right side, fold back the facing edges, and edgestitch the facing to the body.

12. With right sides together, sew the front body to the back body along the side seams, starting 3" (7.5cm) above the bottom hem and going up to the sleeve hems.

french sailor dress

This dress, which I'm showing in a navy-and-white polka-dot silk with a solid white contrast yoke and pleated hem, has a polished *élan* that feels *très* Parisian. The navy buttons give it a true nautical look.

supplies

1¼ yards (1.1m) navy-and-white polka-dot silk
¾ yard (69cm) white silk
Four 18 line buttons

pattern adjustments

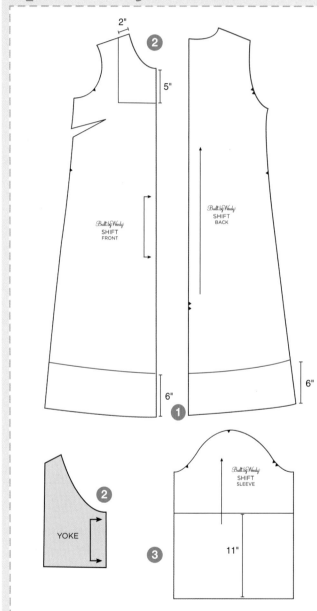

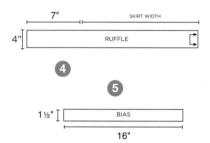

1. Shorten the front and back body length by 6″ (15cm) at the bottom.

2. Make a front yoke by drawing perpendicular lines from points on the shoulder 2″ (5cm) out from the neckline and 5″ (12.5cm) below the center front of the neckline.

3. Shorten the sleeve length by 11″ (28cm) at the bottom.

4. Make a pleated ruffle hem piece measuring 7″ (18cm) longer the than skirt width by 4″ (10cm).

5. Make a bias binding piece measuring 1½″ by 16″ (3.8cm x 40.5cm) to go around the neck opening.

6. Add seam allowances to all pieces.

cutting

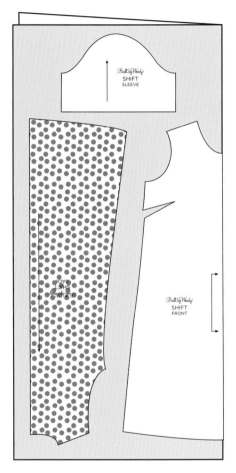

Self: 44" (112cm) wide

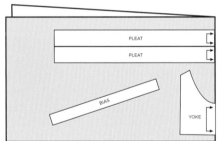

Contrast: 44" (112cm) wide

Hipper Zipper Jumper

Try making this style in denim as a sleeveless jumper. Don't sew the front yoke; instead just cover the entire square neckline with binding. Cut the front pieces so that you have a center front seam, and insert a zipper there for an edgy twist. This makes a super-cute look when layered over a T-shirt (even your boyfriend's ratty one!) or a ruffly blouse.

sewing

1. With right sides together, sew the yoke to the front body neckline.

2. Sew the front darts.

3. With right sides together, sew the front body to the back body pieces at the shoulders.

4. Finish the neckline with bias binding made from the self fabric (the polka-dot silk).

5. With right sides together, sew the back pieces together.

6. With right sides together, sew the sleeve caps to the body armholes.

7. Fold back the sleeve hems 1" (2.5cm) and topstitch.

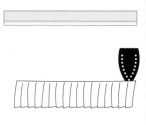

8. Fold back a ½" (13mm) hem along one long edge of the to-be-pleated hem piece and topstitch.

9. Using your fingers, make ¼" (6mm) wide pleats along both hem pieces. Press each pleat.

10. With right sides together, sew one hem piece to the front body. Sew the remaining hem piece to the back body.

11. With right sides together, sew the front body to the back body along the side seams from the pleated hem up to the sleeve hems.

12. Attach the four buttons to the yoke.

deep impact

This fall dress, shown here in red wool, has a striking, seductive silhouette with an Empire waist and dramatic pleat. I also love it layered over a turtleneck with chunky tights and knee-high boots for a seventies-Connecticut-housewife look (if you haven't seen Sigourney Weaver's turn as a glamorous man-eater in *The Ice Storm*, rent it!). Plus, the dress is just as great for summer if you make it in a lightweight cotton.

supplies

2 yards (1.8m) red wool crepe

pattern adjustments

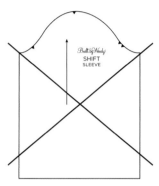

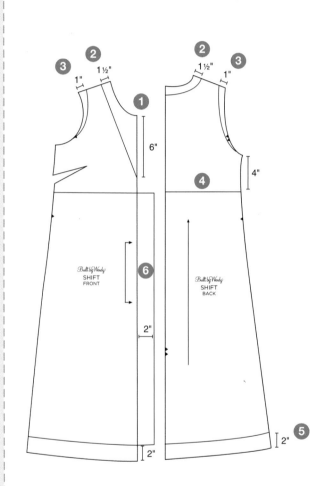

1. Drop the center front neck by 6″ (15cm).

2. Move the front neckline out by 1½″ (3.8cm) at the shoulder seam, and blend to the new center front. Drop the back neckline 1½″ (3.8cm) all around the neckline.

3. Move the armholes in by 1″ (2.5cm) at the shoulder seams and blend close to the armhole notches.

4. Make a horizontal line across the front and back body pieces located 2″ (5cm) above the side seam waist notches.

5. Shorten the skirt pieces by 2″ (5cm) at the bottom.

6. For the front skirt piece, add 2″ (5cm) to the center lower front body (below the horizontal line). Do not add width to the back skirt piece the same; simply cut at the horizontal line.

7. Add seam allowances to all pieces.

cutting

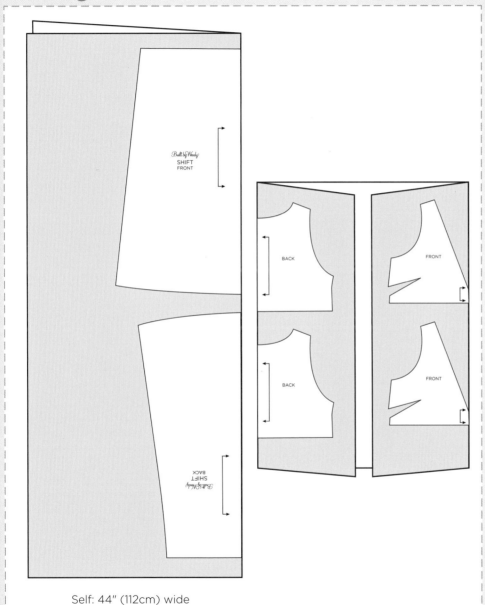

Self: 44" (112cm) wide

Luxe Be a Lady

Why not try making a glam-bohemian version of this dress out of purple silk? Add purple chiffon sleeves for textural contrast and dramatically billowing movement, and apply jewels around the neckline. Since the fabric is smooth, there's no need for a full dress lining; all you need is a neck facing. Instead of a center front pleat, gently gather the skirt at the center front for a softer look.

sewing

1. Sew the darts of the front bodice and self lining pieces.

2. With right sides together, sew the front bodice to the back bodice at the side seams. Do the same for the bodice lining.

3. With right sides together, sew the bodice to the bodice lining around the front neckline, back neckline, and armholes, stopping 2″ (5cm) before you reach the shoulders for each of these seams.

4. Flip the bodice right side out and sew the front to the back at the shoulders. Do the same for the lining.

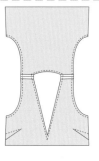

5. Turn the bodice inside out and finish sewing around the neckline and armholes.

6. With right sides together, sew the front and back skirt together at the side seams.

7. Fold back the skirt hem and topstitch 1″.

8. Fold in the front pleat.

9. With right sides together, sew the skirt to the bodice, matching side seam points.

PROJECT 4

rock the boatneck

Fun, bold color-blocking—using four different colors of the same fabric!—is a surefire way to shake up this classic shape.

supplies

¼ yard (23cm) tan cotton

1¼ yard (1.1m) navy cotton

1¼ yard (1.1m) blue cotton

1½ yard (1.4m) red cotton

1 yard (91cm) bias binding

pattern adjustments

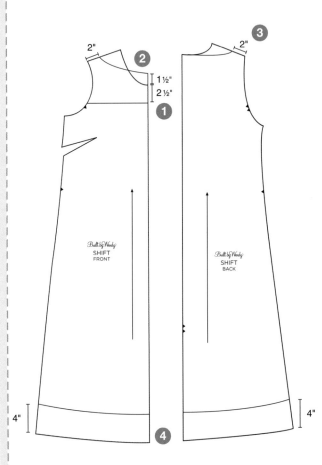

1. Make a horizontal line across the front body piece 2½" (6.5cm) below the center front.

2. Raise the center front neckline by 1½" (3.8cm) and blend to a point along the shoulder 2" (5cm) in from the armhole.

3. Blend the back neckline to a point along the shoulder 2" (5cm) in from the armhole.

4. Shorten the front and back body length by 4" (10cm) at the bottom.

5. Add seam allowances to all pieces.

cutting

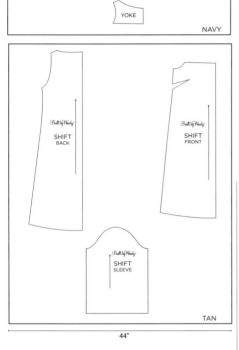

YOKE

NAVY

SHIFT
BACK

SHIFT
FRONT

SHIFT
SLEEVE

TAN

44"

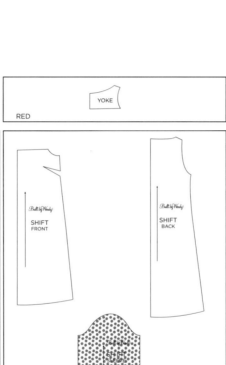

YOKE

RED

SHIFT
FRONT

SHIFT
BACK

BLUE

44"

Self: 44" (112cm) wide

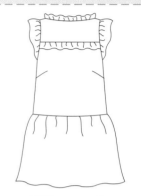

Frill Seeker

Create a totally different, sweet yet chic look by making this dress in black dotted Swiss fabric with a drop waist. Make another horizontal line below the hip (as you did across the chest) to create a skirt part. Slash and spread the lower skirt part widthwise for a flouncy effect. Insert ruffles into the drop waist and yoke seams, and finish the neckline with a ruffle instead of bias binding. There's no need for sleeves; just finish the armholes with—you guessed it—more ruffles. Get ready to ruffle some feathers!

sewing

1. With right sides together, sew the front yokes to the corresponding front body pieces.

2. With right sides together, sew the front body pieces together.

3. Sew the darts.

4. With right sides together, sew the back body pieces together.

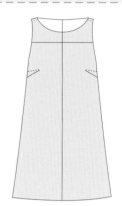

5. With right sides together, sew the front body to the back body at the shoulders.

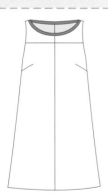

6. Sew bias binding around the neckline to finish it: Fold the strip back inside itself and topstitch.

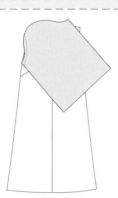

7. With right sides together, sew the sleeve caps to the body armholes.

8. With right sides together, sew the front body to the back body along the side seams from the hem up to the sleeve hems.

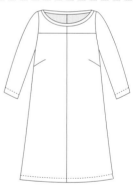

9. Fold back the sleeve hems and skirt hem, and topstitch 1".

about a boy

There's simply nothing quite like a man's shirt on a woman: The classic styling, the crispness of cotton, the casual air, the intrigue of an androgynous silhouette. This dress version has all the timeless details of your boyfriend's shirt, but is even better since it's cut to flatter instead of hanging like a deflated balloon.

supplies

2 yards (1.8m) blue cotton oxford
½ yard (46cm) fusible interfacing
9 white 18 line shirt buttons

pattern adjustments

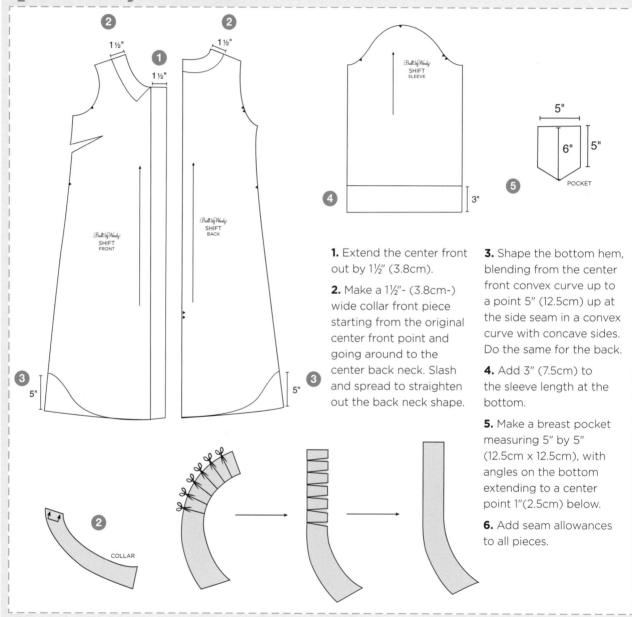

1. Extend the center front out by 1½″ (3.8cm).

2. Make a 1½″- (3.8cm-) wide collar front piece starting from the original center front point and going around to the center back neck. Slash and spread to straighten out the back neck shape.

3. Shape the bottom hem, blending from the center front convex curve up to a point 5″ (12.5cm) up at the side seam in a convex curve with concave sides. Do the same for the back.

4. Add 3″ (7.5cm) to the sleeve length at the bottom.

5. Make a breast pocket measuring 5″ by 5″ (12.5cm x 12.5cm), with angles on the bottom extending to a center point 1″(2.5cm) below.

6. Add seam allowances to all pieces.

cutting

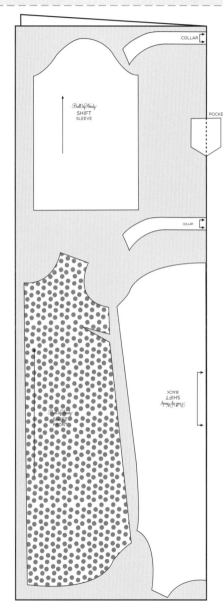

COLLAR

SHIFT
SLEEVE

POCKET

COLLAR

SHIFT
BACK

SHIFT
FRONT

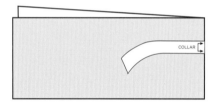

COLLAR

Fusible interfacing: 44"
(112cm) wide

Self: 44" (112cm) wide

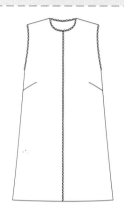

Girls Will Be Girls

For an unexpectedly feminine twist, try making the same dress out of pink cotton or silk. Make the hems straight, and leave off the collar, pocket, sleeves, and front buttonhole extension— just make a simple sheath with a center front seam. Insert a ruffle around the neckline and armholes and along the center front seam. Simply chic!

sewing

1. Iron fusible interfacing to the wrong side of the collar.

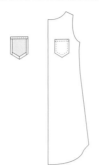

2. Fold back the seam allowances of the pocket, topstitch the top edge, pin it to the front body, and topstitch.

3. Fold back the center front by ½" (13mm) and then fold it another ½" (13mm), and topstitch.

4. With right sides together, sew the collar pieces together around the outer edge, starting and stopping about ½" (13mm) in from the neck seam allowance.

5. With right sides together, sew the front body to the back body at the shoulders.

6. Flip the collar right side out and sew the right side of the undercollar to the right side of the body neckline.

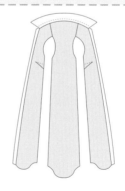

7. Fold in the collar's seam allowance and topstitch around the entire collar, securing it to the body.

8. Sew the darts.

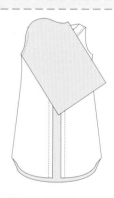

9. With right sides together, sew the sleeve caps to the body armholes.

10. With right sides together, sew the front body to the back body along the side seams from the hem up to the sleeve hems.

11. Fold back the hem ¼" (6mm) and then fold it another ¼" (6mm), and topstitch to make a clean-finish hem.

12. Fold back the sleeve hem by 2" (5cm) and topstitch. Roll up the sleeve to make a cuff.

13. Mark buttonholes every 3" (7.5cm) starting from the top at the center front neck.

14. Attach the buttons and make buttonholes.

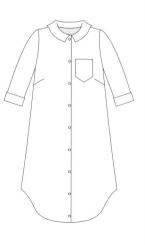

use your illusion

I love *trompe l'oeil*—the art of optical illusion. This mock cardigan dress has a fun, Chanel-chic look that will cause double takes everywhere you go!

supplies

2 yards (1.8m) red wool twill

1½ yards (1.4m) tan wool twill

4 yards (3.7m) black wool trim

3 black 20 line buttons

22" (56cm) red zipper

1 yard (91cm) red wool twill bias binding

pattern adjustments

1. Make a center front piece by blending a line from a point on the neckline 2¾" (7cm) in from the center front to a point 1½" (3.8cm) in from the center front at the bottom edge.

2. Add seam allowances to all pieces.

cutting

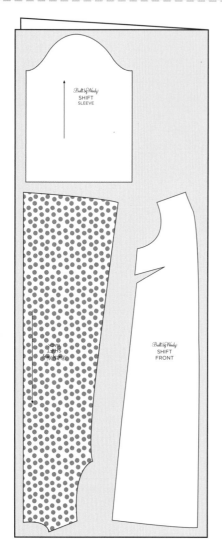

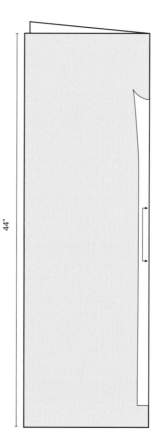

Self: 44" (112cm) wide

Contrast: 44" (112cm) wide

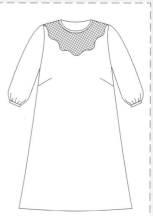

Sheer Genius

Want to reach deeper into your bag of tricks? Apply alternate style lines to make pattern pieces to be cut in contrast fabric. Try making a neck yoke out of lace and a body from green silk for an unforgettable cocktail party dress.

sewing

1. With right sides together, sew the side front pieces to the center front piece.

2. Sew the darts.

3. Topstitch trim over the front seams and horizontally at the front hips for about 5" (12.5cm) for a mock-pocket look. Do a topstitch in the shape of a pocket around the faux pocket trim.

4. With right sides together, sew the back pieces together from the hem to the notch, then baste from the notch to the neck.

5. Insert the zipper in the center back.

6. With right sides together, sew the front body to the back body at the shoulders.

7. Finish the neckline with bias binding. Topstitch trim on top of the bias binding.

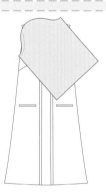

8. With right sides together, sew the sleeve caps to the body armholes.

9. With right sides together, sew the front body to the back body along the side seams from the hem up to the sleeve hems.

sewing

10. Fold back the hem and the sleeve hems 1″ (2.5cm), and topstitch.

11. If desired, attach 3 buttons along one side of the trim, measuring for even spacing.

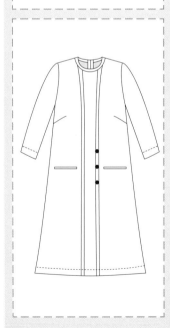

bold shoulders

This unique party dress is the result of layering two one-shoulder dresses in two different fabrics to wear as one complete piece—your wardrobe's *pièce de résistance*! (The layers aren't sewn together, so you can also wear the navy silk layer by itself, but I wouldn't recommend doing so with the sheer lace.)

supplies

2 yards (1.8m) navy silk
2½ yards (2.3m) silver metallic lace

pattern adjustments

2. On the front piece, move the armhole in at the shoulder by 1″ (2.5cm) and blend to the armhole notch. Do the same for the back piece.

3. Move the neckline in at the shoulder by 2″ (5cm) and blend a line to the point where the armhole meets the side seam. Do the same for the back piece.

4. Add seam allowances to all pieces.

5. Cut out the silver metallic lace using the front and back pieces at the full length.

6. Shorten the front and back body length by 3″ (7.5cm) at the bottom.

7. Turn the pattern pieces over and cut the navy silk.

8. Make a 1½″ by 20″ (3.8cm x 51cm) bias binding pattern piece.

1. Trace the front and back pattern pieces onto folded paper so that you are working with a full pattern (not our usual half, since this is an asymmetrical design).

cutting

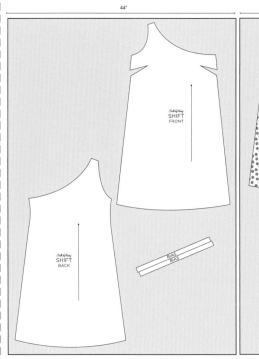

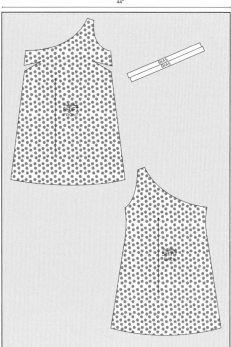

Self: 44" (112cm) wide

Contrast: 44" (112cm) wide

Advanced Geometry

Try making a tiered one-shoulder dress out of an abstract-print fabric. You can even attach a grosgrain ribbon on the strapless side and tie it at the dipping neckline for a different type of asymmetrical neckline.

sewing

1. Sew the darts on the navy silk. Do the same for the lace lining piece.

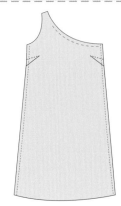

2. With right sides together, sew the front body to the back body along the side seams, one dress layer at a time.

3. Hand-baste the area around the neckline so that it doesn't stretch out during sewing.

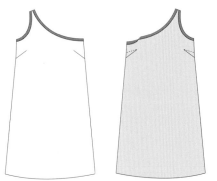

4. Finish the silk dress's neckline and armhole with bias binding, fold the binding inside of the dress, and topstitch. Do the same for the lace lining.

 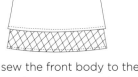

5. With right sides together, sew the front body to the back body at the shoulder, one dress layer at a time.

6. Fold back the hem and topstitch 1". Do the same for the lace lining.

7. Insert the lace lining inside of the navy silk dress.

parachute dress

This tan ripstop cotton number is a great utilitarian look for city streets—sort of *Out of Africa* meets *Private Benjamin*. You'll want to have one on hand in case of a fashion emergency!

supplies

2½ yards (2.3m) tan ripstop cotton
6 yards (5.5m) tan cotton cord

pattern adjustments

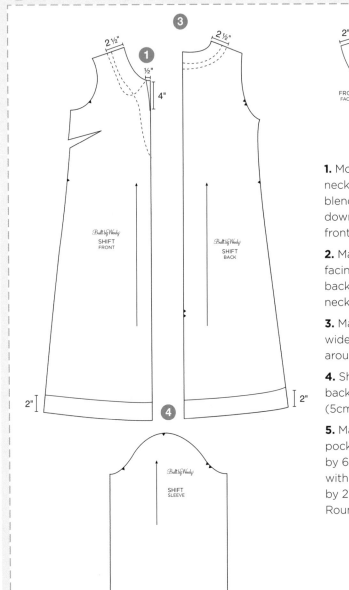

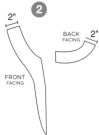

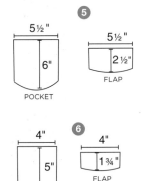

1. Move the center front neck in by ½″ (13mm) and blend to a point 4″ (10cm) down from the center front.

2. Make a 2″- (5cm-) wide facing to go around the back and the front slit neckline.

3. Make a 2½″- (6.5cm-) wide collar piece to go around the neckline.

4. Shorten the front and back body length by 2″ (5cm) at the bottom.

5. Make lower patch pockets measuring 5½″ by 6″ (14cm x 15cm) with flaps measuring 5½″ by 2½″ (14cm x 6.5cm). Round the bottom edge.

6. Make chest patch pockets measuring 4″ by 5″ (10cm x 12.5cm) with flaps measuring 4″ x 1¾″ (10cm x 4.5cm). Round the bottom edge.

7. Add seam allowances to all pieces.

cutting

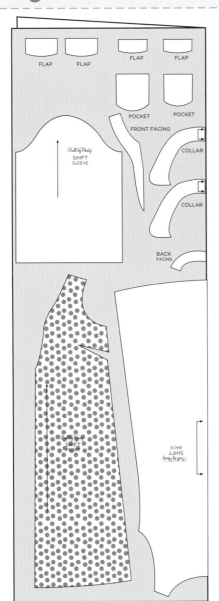

FLAP FLAP FLAP FLAP

POCKET POCKET

FRONT FACING

Built by Wendy
SHIFT
SLEEVE

COLLAR

COLLAR

BACK
FACING

Built by Wendy
SHIFT
FRONT

SHIFT
BACK

Self: 44" (112cm) wide

A Little Romance

Try making the same dress in pretty floral cotton with lace contrast sleeves; insert a bit of elastic at the sleeve hems to make them gather in a similar way. Since this isn't a utilitarian look, you won't want to use pockets, a collar, or cord. Make sure to cut the front on the fold since there is no center front seam.

sewing

1. With right sides together, sew the front pieces together from the bottom of the neckline to 2″ (5cm) above the bottom edge.

2. With right sides together, sew the front body to the back body at the shoulders.

3. Sew the darts.

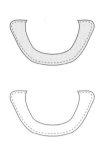

4. With right sides together, sew the collar pieces together around the outer edge, turn the collar right side out, and topstitch around the outer edge.

5. With right sides together, sew the front facing to the back facing at the shoulders.

6. With right sides together, sew the collar to the neckline.

7. With right sides together, sew the facing to the neckline, sandwiching two ½ yard (46cm) lengths of cord inside to come out at the center front.

8. Understitch the facing, then turn the facing to the inside and tack it inside the shoulder seam allowance.

9. With right sides together, sew the pocket flaps together. Turn them right sides out and topstitch.

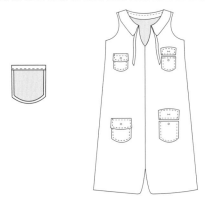

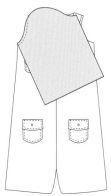

10. Fold back the pocket seam allowances and topstitch them to the front body. Topstitch the pocket flaps' top edges above the pockets. Add buttons and buttonholes to the pockets.

11. With right sides together, sew the sleeve caps to the body armholes.

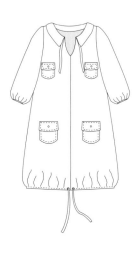

12. Fold back each sleeve hem, topstitch, and insert 1 yard (91cm) of cord.

13. With right sides together, sew the front body to the back body along the side seams from the hem up to just above the hem (left open for the cords) on the sleeve hems.

14. Fold back the hem, topstitch, and insert 3 yards (2.75m) of cord into the casing formed by the hem.

american pastoral

Whether you're hanging out at your farm upstate or hitting the farmers market in the city, this easy dress made from mattress ticking has a vintage-Americana flair that looks anything but hillbillyish.

supplies

2 yards (1.8m) navy-and-natural mattress ticking

Nine 18 line navy buttons

pattern adjustments

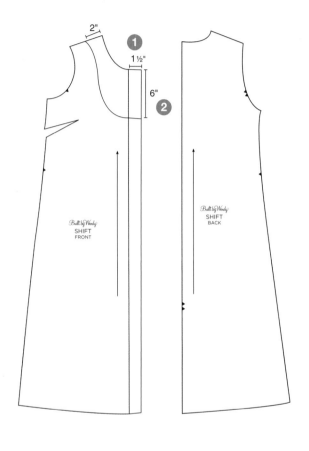

1. Extend the center front by 1½″ (3.8cm).

2. Make a yoke extending 2″ (5cm) out from the neck at the shoulder and blend to a point 6″ (15cm) below the center front neck.

3. Make a mandarin collar piece measuring 19½″ by ½″ (49.5cm x 13mm).

4. Add seam allowances to all pieces.

Into the Woods

For an equally rustic look perfect for cozy fall nights by the fire, try making this dress in plaid flannel with pockets, cuffs, and a yoke in a contrast-color plaid cut on the bias (otherwise, it's too hard to line up the pattern). Big wood buttons add a bit of texture and wit. Note: You'll have to create a facing if you're not making the mandarin collar.

cutting

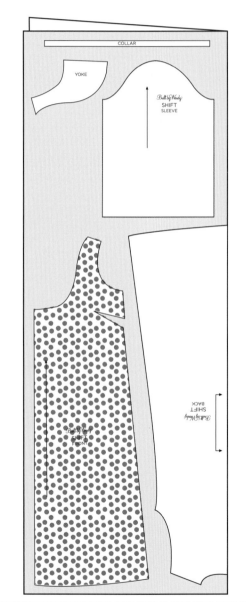

COLLAR

YOKE

Built by Wendy
SHIFT
SLEEVE

Built by Wendy
SHIFT
BACK

Built by Wendy
SHIFT
FRONT

Self: 44" (112cm) wide

sewing

1. With right sides together, sew the front yoke pieces to the front body pieces.

2. With right sides together, sew the front body to the back body at the shoulders.

3. Sew the darts.

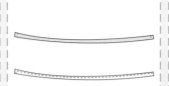

4. With right sides together, sew the sleeve caps to the body armholes.

5. With right sides together, sew the front body to the back body at the side seams from the hem to the sleeve hem.

6. Fold back the sleeve hems 1″ (2.5m) and topstitch. Roll them up to make a cuff.

7. With right sides together, fold the mandarin collar in half lengthwise, sew the ends, turn it right side out, and topstitch around the folded edge.

8. With right sides together, sew the collar to the neckline.

9. Fold the front extension onto the right-hand side of the body, stitch at the neckline, catching the collar into the extension, turn it around, and topstitch from the center front down to the hem. Do the same for the left side.

10. Fold back the hem 1½″ (3.8cm) and topstitch.

11. Sew buttonholes and attach buttons.

CHAPTER 7

THE DIRNDL DRESS

DON'T LET THE FUNNY NAME THROW YOU OFF: This super-adaptable dress pattern offers far more possibilities than just the German peasant frock it's named after. With a fitted bodice, cap sleeves, and a full gathered skirt that hits below the knee, it creates a graceful, womanly silhouette that flatters both extremes of the body-shape spectrum (and everyone in between). For the pear shaped, the folds of the skirt skim the hips and the stomach and accentuate a small waist; the dress also creates an hourglass silhouette on Olive Oyl types. The pattern can be tweaked to create so many different styles that you're sure to be inspired to design a few new ones of your own!

uptown girl

This classic silk LBD—trimmed with white for a *très* French touch—exudes timeless style and grace. The simple T-shirt styling of the bodice keeps the vibe unfussy. You'll feel like Audrey Hepburn the instant you throw it on (though I love it with lace tights and serious heels to give it a bit of a bad-girl twist).

supplies

2 yards (1.8m) black silk satin

1 yard (91cm) white silk satin

1 yard (91cm) ¾" (2cm) wide white satin ribbon

¼ yard (23cm) black interfacing

22" (56cm) black zipper

pattern adjustments

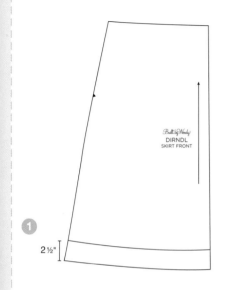

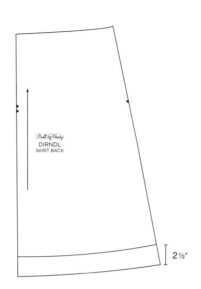

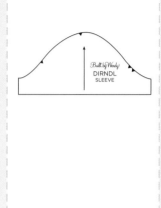

2½"

2½"

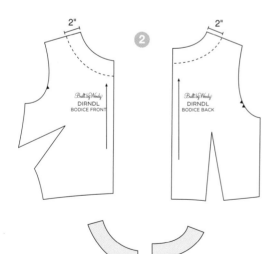

2"

2"

1. Cut out front and back skirt pieces first in the lining fabric, then shorten the front and back skirt pieces by 2½" (6.5cm) at the bottom for the self fabric.

2. Make 2" (5cm) wide front and back neck facing pieces.

3. Add seam allowances to all pieces.

cutting

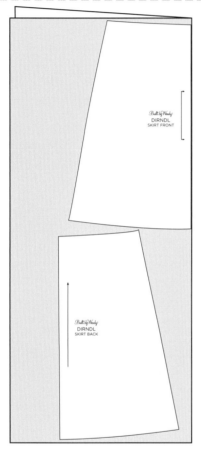

Lining: 44" (112cm) wide

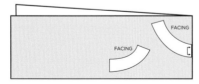

Fusible interfacing: 44" (112cm) wide

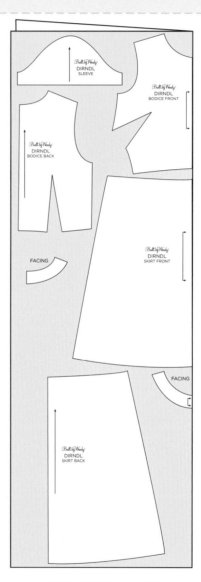

Self: 44" (112cm) wide

Shooting Star Dress

Another fun, cocktail-friendly take on this essential shape is to make it mini-length in dark blue silk and embellish it with rhinestones in a starburst pattern radiating from the neck. You'll leave all the other partygoers starry eyed!

sewing

1. Iron fusible interfacing to the wrong sides of the front and back facings.

2. Sew the front and back bodice darts.

3. With right sides together, sew the front bodice to the back bodice at the shoulders.

4. With right sides together, sew the sleeve caps to the armholes.

5. With right sides together, sew the front bodice to the back bodice at the side seams from the waist up to the sleeve hem.

6. Fold back the sleeve hem 1″ (2.5cm), and topstitch.

7. With right sides together, sew the front skirt piece to the back skirt piece at the side seams. Do the same for the skirt lining.

8. Fold back the skirt and the skirt lining hems by 1″ (2.5cm), and topstitch.

sewing

9. Lay the skirt on top of the skirt lining, right sides up, and gather the skirts together at the waist.

10. With right sides together, sew the bodice to the skirts at the waist.

11. Topstitch the ribbon around the waist seam.

12. With right sides together, sew the back pieces together from the hem to the notch, then baste from the notch to the neck.

13. Insert the zipper.

14. With right sides together, sew the front neck facing to the back neck facing at the side seams.

15. With right sides together, sew the neck facing to the bodice neckline. Understitch around the facing. Turn it to the inside of the dress and tack it to the shoulder seams and zipper tape.

lumberjack dress

Who doesn't love a little lumberjack plaid in wintertime? This formfitting, flattering, feminine twist on the old standby has toggle buttons and not-for-the-boys three-quarter sleeves. It's dangerously cute with tights and boots.

supplies

2½ yards (2.3m) buffalo plaid
¼ yard (23cm) black interfacing
3 toggle closures
22" (56cm) black zipper

pattern adjustments

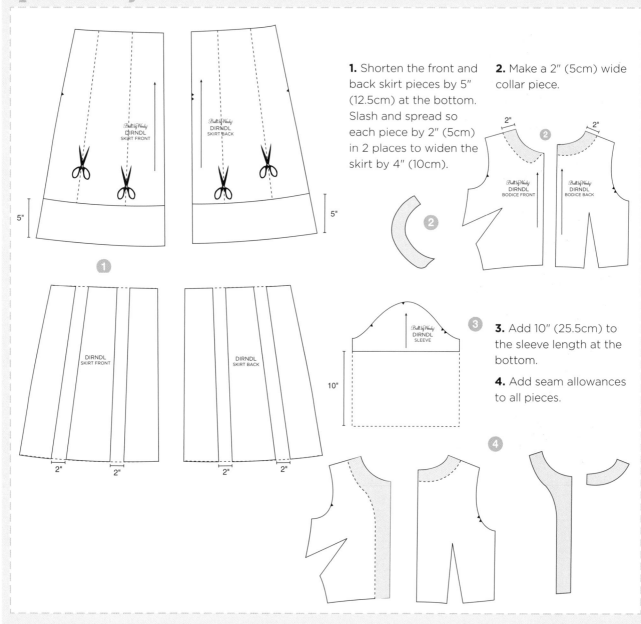

1. Shorten the front and back skirt pieces by 5″ (12.5cm) at the bottom. Slash and spread so each piece by 2″ (5cm) in 2 places to widen the skirt by 4″ (10cm).

2. Make a 2″ (5cm) wide collar piece.

3. Add 10″ (25.5cm) to the sleeve length at the bottom.

4. Add seam allowances to all pieces.

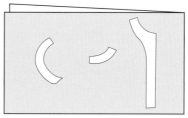

Fusible interfacing: 44"
(112cm) wide

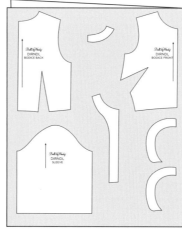

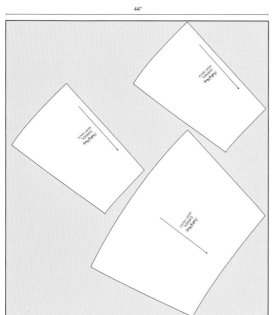

SELF

Self: 44" (112cm) wide

Empress Dress

You can do a complete 180 with this pattern by making it in Chinese red jacquard trimmed with black binding, substituting in a mandarin collar, and swapping cord frog closures (they don't literally look like frogs—they're traditional Chinese knotted cord closures) for the toggles. Add crimson lipstick for a very glamorous after-dark look.

sewing

1. Iron fusible interfacing to the wrong side of the collar.

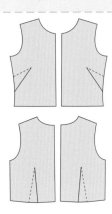

2. Sew the front and back bodice darts.

3. Gather the front and back skirt pieces at the waist. Fold back the skirt hem 1" (2.5cm), and topstitch.

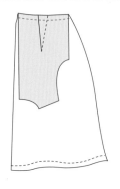

4. With right sides together, sew the back bodice to the back skirt pieces at the waist.

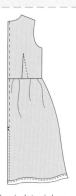

5. With right sides together, sew the back pieces together from the hem to the notch, then baste from the notch to the neck.

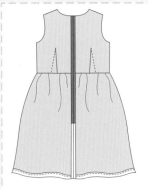

6. Insert the zipper.

7. Fold back center front bodice and topstitch.

8. With right sides together, sew the front skirt to the front bodice at the waist.

9. With right sides together, sew the front bodice to the back bodice at the shoulders.

10. With right sides together, sew the sleeve caps to the armholes.

11. With right sides together, sew the front to the back along the side seams from the hem to the sleeve hem.

12. Fold back the sleeve hem 3" (7.5cm), and topstitch. Roll up the sleeve to form a cuff.

13. With right sides together, sew the collar pieces together around the outer edge. Turn them right side out and topstitch around the edge.

14. Sew the collars to the right side of the neckline, stitching along the inside edge.

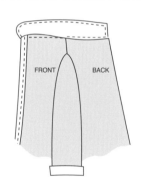

FRONT   BACK

15. Sandwich the neck seam inside of the collar and topstitch around the neck edge of the collar.

16. Attach the toggles along the center front bodice.

PROJECT 3

valentine dress

This flirtatious two-tone mock-bustier dress has style lines along the bust that suggest the look of lingerie, enhancing your curves together with the nipped waist and romantic double-layer flutter sleeves. Comfy yet dressy, it's a great option for a date—and a surefire way to give a boyish figure a boost.

supplies

2½ yards (2.3m) red cotton
1½ yards (1.4m) hot-pink cotton
¼ yard (23cm) interfacing
22" (56cm) pink zipper

pattern adjustments

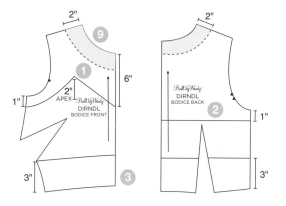

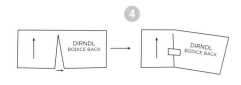

1. Mark a point on the front side seam down 1" (2.5cm) from the armhole, and mark a point 6" (15cm) down the center front. Draw a peaked line from side seam to 2" (5cm) above bust apex to center front.

2. Mark a point at the back side seam 1" (2.5cm) below the armhole and draw a horizontal line to the center back.

3. Raise the front and back waist seams on the bodice by 3" (7.5cm).

4. Remove the back bodice dart by slashing the dart and taping it closed. Make 2"- (5cm-) wide front and back neck facing pieces.

pattern adjustments

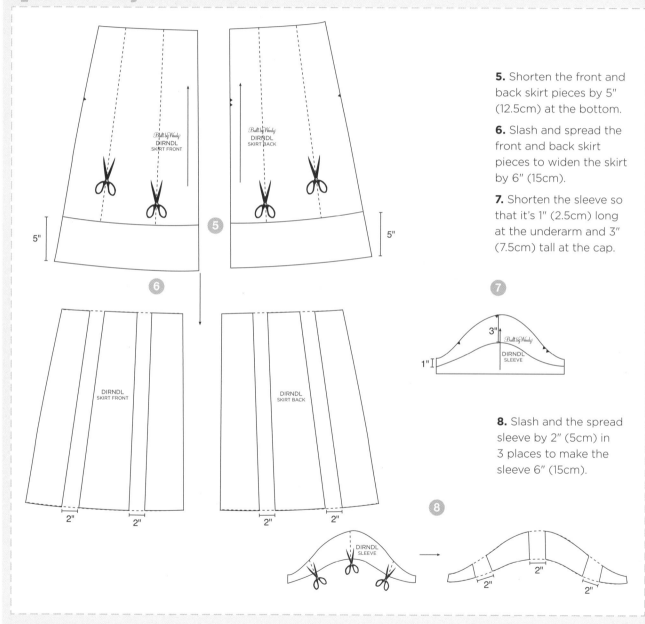

5. Shorten the front and back skirt pieces by 5" (12.5cm) at the bottom.

6. Slash and spread the front and back skirt pieces to widen the skirt by 6" (15cm).

7. Shorten the sleeve so that it's 1" (2.5cm) long at the underarm and 3" (7.5cm) tall at the cap.

8. Slash and the spread sleeve by 2" (5cm) in 3 places to make the sleeve 6" (15cm).

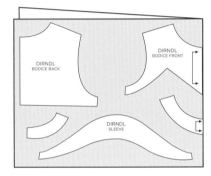

Contrast: 44" (112cm) wide

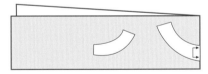

Fusible interfacing: 44"
(112cm) wide

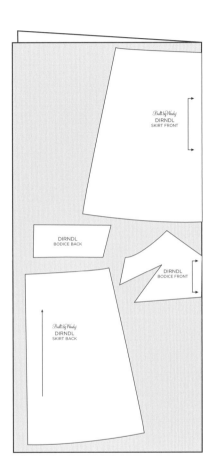

Self: 44"w (112cm) wide

Afternoon Delight

Done up in yellow gauze with white trim, the sleeveless summer version of this dress is dreamy in a seventies-inspired, *Virgin Suicides* sort of way. Just leave off the upper bodice part and sleeves and add straps of white bias binding, which you can also use to trim all the edges. Add a few longer layers of fabric for extra movement. Perfect for a lazy picnic in a field of daisies!

1. Iron fusible interfacing to the wrong sides of the front and back facings.

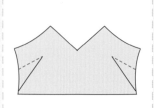

2. Sew the front bodice darts.

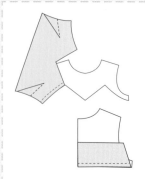

3. With right sides together, sew the front bodice to the upper front piece. Sew the back bodice to the upper back pieces.

4. With right sides together, sew the front bodice to the back bodice at the shoulders.

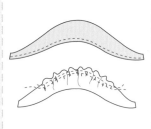

5. With right sides together, sew the sleeves pieces together at the hem. Turn them right side out and gather the sleeve caps.

6. With right sides together, sew the sleeve caps to the armholes.

7. With right sides together, sew the front bodice to the back bodice along the side seams from the waist to the sleeve hem.

8. With right sides together, sew the skirt front to the skirt backs along the side seams.

9. Fold back the skirt hem 1″ (2.5cm), and topstitch. Gather the skirt at the waist.

10. With right sides together, sew the bodice to the skirt at the waist.

11. With right sides together, sew the back pieces together from the hem to the notch, then baste from the notch to the neck.

12. Insert the zipper.

13. With right sides together, sew the front neck facing to the back neck facing at the side seams.

14. With right sides together, sew the neck facing to the bodice neckline. Understitch around the facing. Turn it to the inside of the dress and tack it to the shoulder seams and the zipper tape.

bohemian rhapsody

There's nothing sweeter in summer than a full-length sundress. With a dramatic tie-front deep-V neck and floral ribbon trim at the hem, this floral cotton dress can take you from garden weddings to outdoor rock festivals, depending on how you style it.

supplies

3 yards (2.75m) printed cotton lawn

1 yard (91cm) contrasting solid cotton lawn

½ yard (46cm) fusible interfacing

3 yards (2.75m) 1"- (2.5cm-) wide floral ribbon trim

22" (56cm) zipper

pattern adjustments

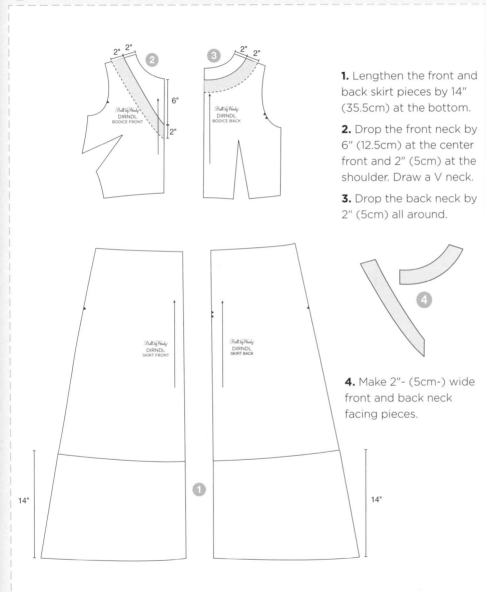

1. Lengthen the front and back skirt pieces by 14″ (35.5cm) at the bottom.

2. Drop the front neck by 6″ (12.5cm) at the center front and 2″ (5cm) at the shoulder. Draw a V neck.

3. Drop the back neck by 2″ (5cm) all around.

4. Make 2″- (5cm-) wide front and back neck facing pieces.

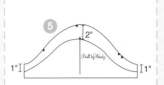

5. Make a cap sleeve that is 1″ (2.5cm) long at the armhole and 2″ (5cm) tall at the cap.

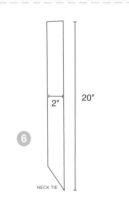

6. Make a neck tie piece measuring 20″ (51cm) long and 2″ (5cm) wide. Make the tip an angled point.

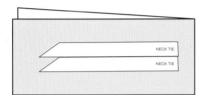

Contrast: 44" (112cm) wide

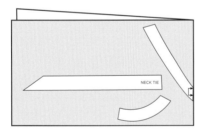

Fusible interfacing: 44" (112cm) wide

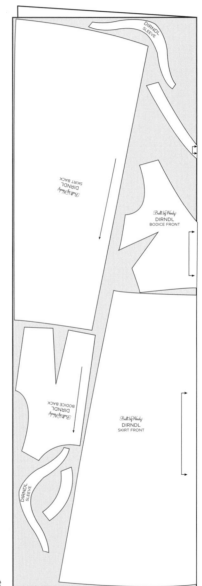

Self: 44" (112cm) wide

Hello, Sailor!

The same use of contrast works equally well in black and white cotton for a fun, nautical-inspired look. To make this version, simply shorten the pattern to a saucy mini length and add a contrast yoke, framing the shape with trim.

sewing

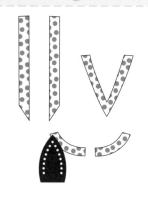

1. Iron fusible interfacing to the wrong sides of the front and back facings and the neck tie pieces.

2. Sew the front and back bodice darts.

3. With right sides together, sew the front bodice to the back bodice at the shoulders.

4. With right sides together, sew the sleeve caps to the armholes.

5. With right sides together, sew the front bodice to the back bodice along the side seams from the waist to the sleeve hem.

6. Fold back the sleeve hem ½" (13mm), and topstitch.

7. With right sides together, sew the front skirt piece to the back skirt pieces along the side seams.

8. Gather the skirt at the waist. Fold back the skirt hem 1" (2.5cm), and topstitch the ribbon around the hem.

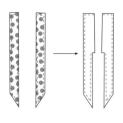

9. With right sides together, sew the neck tie pieces together around the outer edge, leaving a front v-neck length open. Turn them right sides out and topstitch around the edge.

sewing

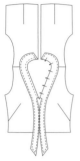

10. Pin or baste the neck tie to the right side of the neckline.

11. With right sides together, sew the front facings to the back facings at the shoulder seams.

12. With right sides together, sew the facing to the neckline, sandwiching the neck tie into the seam. Understitch around the facing.

13. With right sides together, sew the bodice to the skirt at the waist.

14. With right sides together, sew the back pieces together from the hem to the notch, then baste from the notch to the neck.

15. Insert the zipper.

16. Tack the back facing to the zipper tape and the shoulder seams.

PROJECT 5

lolita dress

I can picture a doe-eyed Parisian *ingenue*, circa 1958, in this slightly retro, completely adorable dress. With a sunny yellow polka-dot body, cord-trimmed contrast yoke, and sweet buttons, it's equal parts sass and class.

supplies

2 yards (1.8m) yellow dotted swiss
½ yard (46cm) white cotton piqué
¼ yard (23cm) interfacing
2 yards (1.8m) black piping
2 small 18 line black buttons
22" (56cm) yellow zipper
Store-bought binding

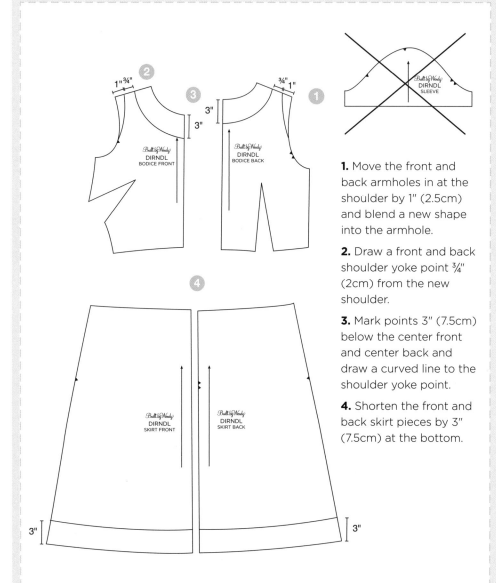

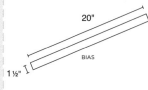

1. Move the front and back armholes in at the shoulder by 1" (2.5cm) and blend a new shape into the armhole.

2. Draw a front and back shoulder yoke point ¾" (2cm) from the new shoulder.

3. Mark points 3" (7.5cm) below the center front and center back and draw a curved line to the shoulder yoke point.

4. Shorten the front and back skirt pieces by 3" (7.5cm) at the bottom.

5. Make a 1½" by 20" (3.8cm x 51cm) strip for bias binding.

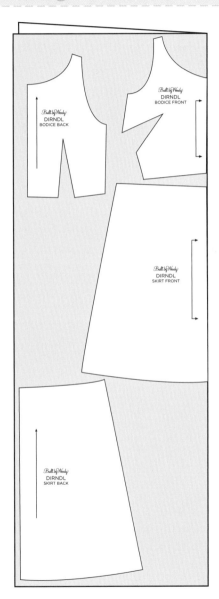

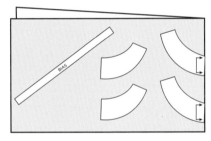

Self: 44" (112cm) wide

Contrast: 44" (112cm) wide

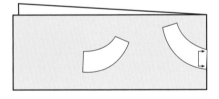

Fusible interfacing: 44" (112cm) wide

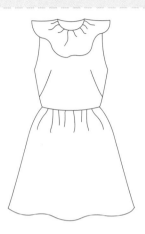

Color Purple

For a cute party dress that's so easy to make, try a different version of this dress in rich purple silk. Just slash and spread the neck yoke piece to make it into a ruffle around the neck. Add a few inches all around so that it reaches out slightly over the shoulder.

1. Iron fusible interfacing to the wrong sides of the front and back yoke facings.

2. Sew the front and back bodice darts.

3. With right sides together, sew the front bodice to the back bodice at the shoulders.

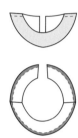

4. With right sides together, sew the front yoke to the back yoke at the shoulders.

5. Sew piping with the raw edge along the outside raw edge of the yoke.

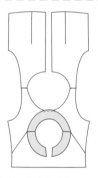

6. With right sides together, sew the yoke to the bodice, sandwiching the seam allowance attached to the piping into the seam.

7. With right sides together, sew bias binding around each armhole, fold it inside of the armhole, and topstitch.

8. With right sides together, sew the front bodice to the back bodice along the side seams from the waist up to the armholes.

9. With right sides together, sew the front skirt piece to the back skirt pieces at the side seams.

10. Fold back the skirt hem 1″ (2.5cm), and topstitch. Gather the skirt at the waist.

11. With right sides together, sew the bodice to the skirt at the waist.

12. With right sides together, sew the backs together from the hem to the notch, then baste from the notch to the neck.

13. Insert the zipper.

14. With right sides together, sew the front facing to the back facings at the shoulder seams.

15. With right sides together, sew the facing to the neckline. Understitch around the facing, and turn to the inside.

16. Tack the back facing to the zipper tape and at the shoulder seams.

17. Attach the buttons onto the center front yoke.

tea dress

With a dropped black collar, three-quarter-length sleeves, and decorative buttons, this peach silk stunner has a very romantic, very 1930s look that makes me think of literary types sipping Earl Grey at a Bloomsbury book party.

supplies

2½ yards (2.3m) peach silk

1 yard (91cm) black silk

½ yard (46cm) white interfacing

3 small 18 line black buttons

22" (56cm) peach zipper

pattern adjustments

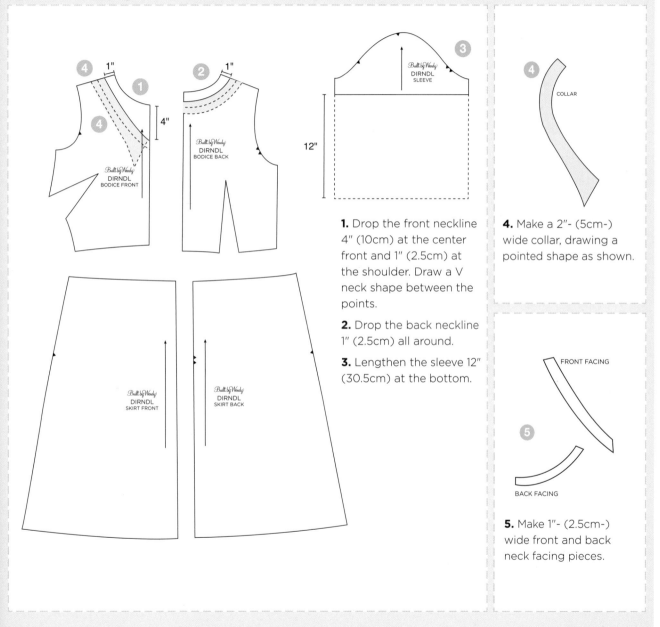

1. Drop the front neckline 4″ (10cm) at the center front and 1″ (2.5cm) at the shoulder. Draw a V neck shape between the points.

2. Drop the back neckline 1″ (2.5cm) all around.

3. Lengthen the sleeve 12″ (30.5cm) at the bottom.

4. Make a 2″- (5cm-) wide collar, drawing a pointed shape as shown.

5. Make 1″- (2.5cm-) wide front and back neck facing pieces.

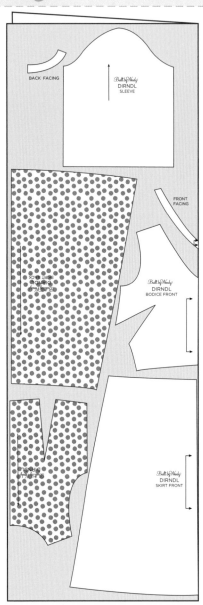

Self: 44" (112cm) wide

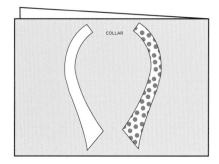

Contrast: 44" (112cm) wide

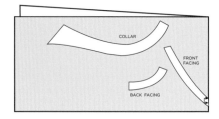

Fusible interfacing: 44" (112cm) wide

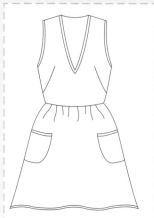

V 2.0

Try making a simple V-neck minidress version of this dress in bright fuchsia linen. Leave off the sleeves and collar and cover all edges with bias binding—you can even try a contrast color such as red or navy for the binding and add some big patch pockets. Pair it with brightly colored flats for a playful, arty Marimekko vibe!

sewing

1. Iron fusible interfacing to the wrong sides of the front and back facing pieces and the collar.

2. Sew the front and back bodice darts.

3. With right sides together, sew the front bodice to the back bodice at the shoulders.

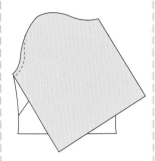

4. With right sides together, sew the sleeve caps to the armholes.

5. With right sides together, sew the front bodice to the back bodice at the side seams from the waist up to the sleeve hems.

6. Fold back the sleeve hems 2″ (5cm), and topstitch. Roll up the sleeves to form a cuff.

7. With right sides together, sew the front skirt piece to the back skirt pieces along the side seams.

8. Fold back the skirt hem 1″ (2.5cm), and topstitch. Gather the skirt at the waist.

sewing

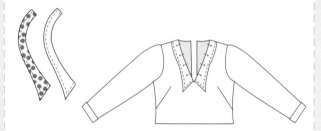

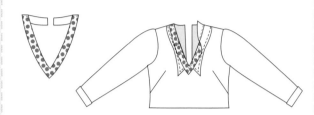

9. With right sides together, sew the collar pieces together around the outer edge. Turn them right side out and topstitch around the outer edge.

10. Pin the collar to the right side of the neckline.

11. With right sides together, sew the front facings to the back facings at the shoulder seams.

12. With right sides together, sew the facing to the neckline, sandwiching the collar into the seam. Understitch around the facing, and turn to the inside.

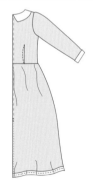

13. With right sides together, sew the bodice to the skirt pieces at the waist.

14. With right sides together, sew the back pieces together from the hem to the notch, then baste from the notch to the neck.

15. Insert the zipper.

16. Tack the back facing to the zipper tape and at the shoulder seams.

17. Attach the buttons onto the center front bodice.

PROJECT 7

hothouse flowers

This bold floral cotton dress is anything but innocent, thanks to its lace trim, deep-V crossover neckline, and sexy open sides. Finish it off with heels for summer cocktails or an *al fresco* dinner date.

supplies

2 yards (1.8m) floral batiste
4 yards (3.7m) 1"- (2.5cm-) wide black lace trim
1 yard (91cm) ½"- (13mm-) wide black elastic

pattern adjustments

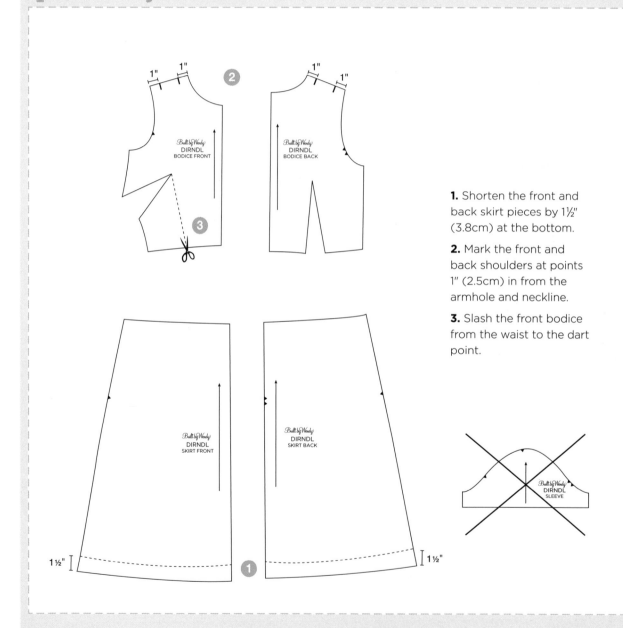

1. Shorten the front and back skirt pieces by 1½″ (3.8cm) at the bottom.

2. Mark the front and back shoulders at points 1″ (2.5cm) in from the armhole and neckline.

3. Slash the front bodice from the waist to the dart point.

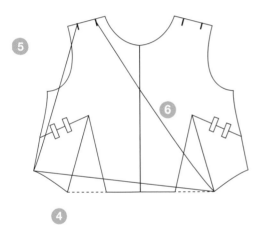

4. Close out the bust dart line by folding it up from the slashed waist point and taping it closed. The dart is now on the waist. Make the front bodice into a full pattern piece.

5. Draw new front and back side seams from the shoulder to the waist.

6. Draw a wrap front line from the shoulder diagonally to the outer leg of the opposite new waist dart.

7. Draw the back neckline from the 1" (2.5cm) mark around the neckline to a point 1" (2.5cm) below the center back.

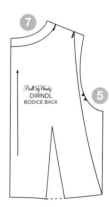

Built by Wendy
DIRNDL
BODICE BACK

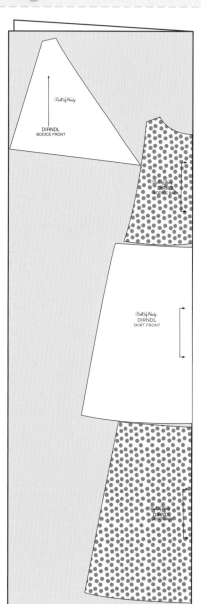

DIRNDL
BODICE FRONT

DIRNDL
BODICE BACK

DIRNDL
SKIRT FRONT

DIRNDL
SKIRT BACK

Self: 44″ (112cm) wide

That's a Wrap

Using this pattern as a basic wrap dress (sans open sides) in colorful African printed cotton makes for a super-fun look. This shape can also be very modern when you make it in a solid color. Since the silhouette is so basic and flattering, it's a great way to test the waters with some more expensive fabrics.

sewing

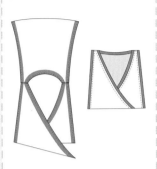

1. With right sides together, sew the front bodice to the back bodice at the shoulders.

2. With right sides together, sew the lace trim to the neckline and the armholes. Turn the lace to its right side and topstitch.

3. With right sides together, sew the front skirt piece to the front bodice pieces at the waist seam. Sew the back skirt to the back bodice.

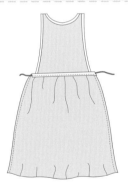

4. Topstitch the waist seam to the skirt, creating a tunnel. Insert elastic into the tunnel. The elastic's length should equal your waist measurement. Cut the elastic in half. Insert one half of the elastic into

back waist tunnel and insert the other half of elastic into the front waist tunnel.

5. With right sides together, sew the front skirt piece to the back skirt piece at the side seams.

6. With right sides together, sew the lace trim to the skirt hem. Turn the lace to its right side and topstitch.

tennis, anyone?

With a flattering deep U-neck, contrast trim, and a D-ring belt, this fun cotton frock has a vintage-seventies meets prep-school vibe that's far too cute to save for the courts. Choose your own iron-on appliqué logo for a finishing touch that's totally ace!

supplies

2 yards (1.8m) white cotton piqué

4 yards (3.7m) red store-bought bias binding

3 yards (2.75m) 1"- (2.5cm-) wide striped grosgrain ribbon

22" (56cm) white zipper

D-ring belt buckle

Small iron-on appliqué

pattern adjustments

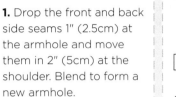

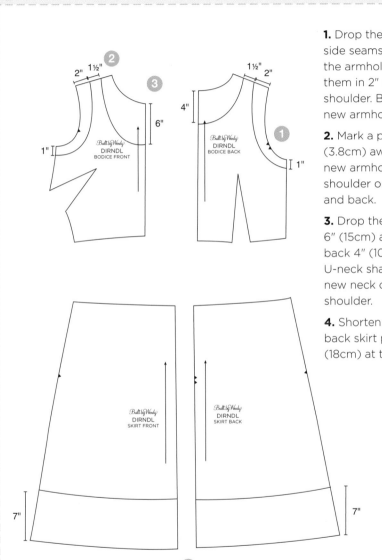

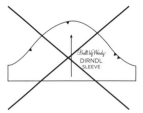

1. Drop the front and back side seams 1″ (2.5cm) at the armhole and move them in 2″ (5cm) at the shoulder. Blend to form a new armhole.

2. Mark a point 1½″ (3.8cm) away from the new armhole at the shoulder on both the front and back.

3. Drop the center front 6″ (15cm) and the center back 4″ (10cm). Draw a U-neck shape up to the new neck opening at the shoulder.

4. Shorten the front and back skirt pieces by 7″ (18cm) at the bottom.

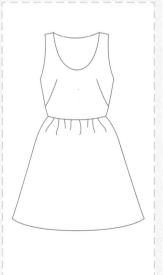

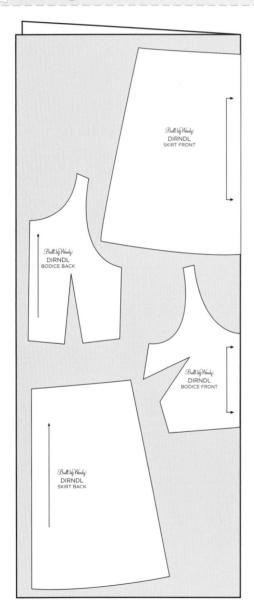

Built by Wendy
DIRNDL
SKIRT FRONT

Built by Wendy
DIRNDL
BODICE BACK

Built by Wendy
DIRNDL
BODICE FRONT

Built by Wendy
DIRNDL
SKIRT BACK

Self: 44" (112cm) wide

Fiesta Dress

Whipped up in fine solid-colored fabric, this voluminous mini silhouette is also perfect for parties. I love the idea of making a sexy Cinco de Mayo dress in a cherry-red silk/cotton blend with dramatic frills attached around the neck and hem. You could even take it black-tie by making it in black silk satin and adding lace tights and heels, or maybe a rhinestone belt. Cheers!

sewing

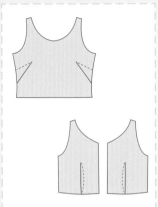

1. Sew front and back bodice darts.

2. With right sides together, sew the front bodice to the back bodice at the shoulders.

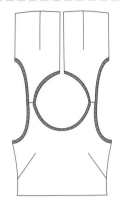

3. Attach bias binding around the neckline and the armholes.

4. With right sides together, sew the front bodice to the back bodice at the side seams.

5. Topstitch the striped ribbon in a vertical line onto the right side of the front skirt piece.

6. With right sides together, sew the front skirt to the back skirt pieces at the side seams.

7. Gather the waist. And attach bias binding around the skirt hem.

8. With right sides together, sew the bodice to the skirt at the waist.

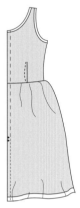

9. With right sides together, sew the back skirt pieces together from the hem to the notch, then baste from the notch to the neck.

10. Insert the zipper.

11. Iron the small appliqué onto the chest.

12. Attach the striped ribbon to the belt buckle.

CHAPTER 8

RECYCLING

FROM RAGS TO DRESSES

WITH ALL THE TECHNIQUES YOU'VE LEARNED IN THIS BOOK, YOU CAN DO MORE THAN JUST MAKE NEW DRESSES—YOU CAN MAKE OLD CLOTHES INTO NEW DRESSES!

We all know the importance of being eco-friendly, but reusing unwanted clothes is also wallet-friendly—and, as a big bonus, it can really kick your creativity up a notch, sparking new design ideas in the process. So many secondhand pieces have great components like fabric or trim that are impossible to replicate and a great way to add personality to your designs. The prissiest blouse could have cool lace trim, and the floral sheets from your childhood bedroom just might make a sweet sundress. So dig through the Goodwill bins, the basement, or the very back of your closet, and give a couple of these ideas a try. It's cheap, it's fun, and it's an excellent way for beginners to get comfortable with sewing dresses before taking the plunge into the project chapters.

alter ego
CHANGING FIT

We've all had that frustrating thrift-store moment when we find an amazing dress that happens to fit horrendously. Now that you're a fit expert, even garments you once thought were untouchable are fair game. Wondering what to do with your frumpy full-length bridesmaid dress? Hem it into a fun mini (even seafoam green isn't so bad, if the dress is short and sweet). Found an eighties' dress with ridiculously poufy, padded-shoulder ruched sleeves? Chop them off, and finish the edges with some cute trim. Bored by your old T-shirt dresses? Add some ruffle trim around a plain neckline. And now that you have pattern pieces that fit, you can even lay them on top of something way too big (like a men's shirt) and cut it into your favorite shape.

girl, deconstructed
REPURPOSING FABRIC

You don't have to spend a fortune on fabric to make the patterns in this book—you can also use old garments or even home textiles. Cut apart old clothing like the big floral muumuu you bought in Hawaii, or make use of a cute embroidered tablecloth or bold printed curtains from a garage sale. Just lay your pattern pieces on top of the fabric as you would for the store-bought variety, and cut and sew. Old garments can also be used to form entire components of the dresses in this book (or new ones you invent). For instance, maybe you've found a long skirt with a cool embellished hem detail. Why not chop off the bottom half and gather it to be joined with a fitted bodice (or your cropped black baby tee from 1993)? This is also a great technique to keep in mind for those moments when you fall in love with the fabric of an old dress but find that it's too small to re-fit to your body. You can always use the top half of a too-short dress as a bodice, or borrow some of the fabric and add it to your design as a decorative yoke or trim.

i'm in pieces
BITS AND PIECES

Call me a pack rat, but I firmly believe that even the smallest scrap of fabric may someday be useful for something. Old clothing is a gold mine for great trims, the kind of detailed doodads they just don't make anymore. Before throwing away that itchy old cardigan, for example, make sure to cut off those great carved jade buttons. You can also cut off collars you like and sew them onto new dresses. I also always stay on the lookout for great pieces of lace that can be inset into a new dress yoke or collar (look for old frilly gowns or even vintage lingerie). You can make appliqués out of large fabric print parts, such as flower shapes or graphic designs, to punch up an LBD. Or if you're really feeling resourceful (and ambitious), push the recycling concept to the next level by taking several garments, cutting them into 3" (7.5cm) squares, and making a madras-style patchwork dress!

Resources

Your local fabric store isn't the only place to shop for supplies. The Web has a world of unique offerings to help you make the perfect dress. Here are a few of my favorite online sites for supplies and materials—and, just as often, inspiration!

ANTIQUE FABRIC
If you really want to make your dress special, check out this site's beautiful old appliqués and sweet vintage prints. Even if you can't find enough material for a dress, it's great to keep in mind for yokes, pockets, or other pieces.
3713 Woody Drive
Boise, ID 83703
www.antiquefabric.com

B & J FABRICS
A popular brick-and-mortar store in NYC for higher-end European fabrics as well as the basics.
525 Seventh Avenue, 2nd Floor
New York, NY 10018
212-354-8150
www.bandjfabrics.com

CLOTILDE
A staple site of mine for sewing supplies—presser feet, needles, you name it.
P.O. Box 7500
Big Sandy, TX 75755
800-772-2891
www.clotilde.com

EBAY
A gold mine for one-of-a-kind vintage fabric, as well as cut-price supplies and machinery. If you want it, it's probably on here somewhere!
www.ebay.com

FABRIC TALES
This site specializes in Japanese fabrics and trims with vibrant color and detail. The patterned cords, ribbons, and beads are also super-inspiring.
1-11 Nakahama-cho
Nishinomiya City
Hyogo
662-0952 JAPAN
www.fabrictales.com

GORGEOUS FABRICS
A site beloved by sewing bloggers for its fun, colorful prints and plaids aplenty.
617-797-5466
www.gorgeousfabrics.com

HANCOCK FABRICS
This national chain, found in most cities, sells a wide array of fabrics as well as essential extras like interfacing. Shop online, or check the website to find a store near you.
877-FABRICS
www.hancockfabrics.com

HEIRLOOM IMPORTS
A fantastic source for Liberty fabrics—traditional but never stodgy British florals that will class up any dress. Check the website for a list of Liberty fabrics resellers throughout the United States.
888-390-2119
www.heirloomimports.com

JO-ANN FABRIC AND CRAFT STORES
An old standby, this chain found throughout the United States stocks a variety of fabrics and trims. Shop online, or check the website to find a store near you.
888-739-4120
www.joann.com

LANETZ LIVING
This site sells loads of amazing vintage patterns—use them to add elements to the patterns in this book, or simply browse for inspiration!
www.lanetzliving.com

M&J TRIMMING
Whether it's piping, ribbon, buttons, or appliqués, you'll find plenty of bells and whistles here to make your design unique.
1008 Sixth Avenue
New York, NY 10018
800-9-MJTRIM
www.mjtrim.com

MOOD FABRICS
As seen in Project Runway—*need I say more? One of the best sources for designer-caliber specialty fabrics.*
225 West 37th Street, 3rd Floor
New York, NY 10018
212-730-5003
www.moodfabrics.com

STEINLAUF AND STOLLER
A New York City–based brick-and-mortar store for professional-quality trims and supplies, including specialty doodads such as webbing, belt backing, and lingerie sliders.
239 West 39th Street
New York, NY 10018
877-869-0321
www.steinlaufandstoller.com

TESSUTI FABRICS
Based in Australia, this online shop with five brick-and-mortar locations sells fabrics bought from the world's top designers.
110 Commonwealth Street
Surry Hills
Sydney
AUSTRALIA
+61 2 9211 5536
www.tessuti-shop.com

VOGUE FABRICS
I grew up going to the Evanston, Illinois, branch of this Chicago-area mini-chain with my mom, and all of my first projects were made from fabrics found here. It's still a great resource for all sorts of fabrics, many offered wholesale.
718–732 Main Street
Evanston, IL 60202
800-433-4313
www.voguefabricsstore.com

Glossary

appliqué A decorative motif to be stitched or ironed on to a dress. You can make your own by cutting out components of old clothing.

backstitch A few stitches in reverse, sewn at the beginning and end of a seam, to secure the threads. Most machines have a button to activate this automatically, or you can do it by hand by turning your hand wheel away from you.

basting stitch A stitch of long length used not to join seams permanently, but to secure fabric in preparation for joining. This stitching is often removed after sewing, but not always.

bias The imaginary line formed at a 45-degree angle from the lengthwise and crosswise grains of woven fabric. This is where fabric stretches the most.

bias binding Also known as bias tape. A thin strip of fabric cut on the bias, used to envelop the raw edge of a hem or seam. It can be bought pre-packaged or be homemade from your own fabric and scraps. A bias tape maker helps speed that process.

blind hem A hem that is virtually invisible from the outside of a garment because the thread only pricks the surface occasionally. A special foot is required to accomplish this. Not recommended for beginners.

bobbin A tiny spool inserted inside the machine, usually underneath the needle hole, that holds thread. The bobbin thread links with the needle thread to form each stitch.

bodice The top part of a dress, for the torso; as opposed to the skirt. Some dresses (such as the shift) do not have a separate bodice and skirt but rather have one body piece in front and back.

color-blocking A design and sewing technique in which different components of a dress are made with different colors or fabrics.

crosswise grain The direction of fabric weave that runs from selvage to selvage, or "horizontally." Also known as the weft.

dart A small pie-shaped marking on a pattern that is sewed into a tuck to give shape to a pattern to better fit the contours of the body.

drop waist A dress waistline style in which the bodice ends and skirt begins at a point below the natural waist, such as at the hips.

edgestitch A line of stitching run extremely close to a folded edge or a seam line. Produces a neater, dressier look and is usually sewn with a shorter stitch length.

Empire waist A skirt waistline that starts just below the bust.

epaulet A military-style tab, usually found on shoulders, that can serve a decorative or practical purpose (as in holding up rolled sleeves).

eyelet A small metal ring or grommet edging a hole in fabric through which ribbon or cord is threaded. Can also refer to a type of fabric with decorative holes in it.

facing Pieces that are mirror images of pattern pieces. Commonly used to finish openings such as necklines, front shirt openings, and armholes. Linings are also facings.

folding In patternmaking, a technique in which the pattern size is reduced from within, rather than by subtracting from hems or side seams.

grainline Generally speaking, this refers to the lengthwise grain—the direction of the weave that runs parallel to the selvage and the most important and strongest direction of the weave.

grainline arrows These mark the direction of the grainline on patterns to indicate where on the fabric the pattern pieces should be placed in relation to the grainline.

hem A common method of finishing a raw edge by turning it under twice and stitching.

interfacing A special layer of fabric, not visible from the outside, joined to the back of fabric to support delicate and detailed areas such as collars, cuffs, and pockets. Comes in sew-on and fusible varieties; fusible interfacing is simply ironed to the back of the fabric.

lengthwise grain The direction of fabric weave that runs parallel to the selvage, or "vertically," and is the strongest direction of the fabric. Also known as the warp.

Glossary

muslin Usually made of cotton, this is an inexpensive fabric used to make test garments before sewing with more precious material. Also refers to the test garment itself.

nap The raised surface of a fabric which changes appearance when brushed or viewed from different angles. Napped fabrics, unlike regular fabrics, must always be cut in the same direction.

notions Everything you use to sew that isn't fabric or trim—needles, thread, interfacing, buttons, zippers, and the like.

one-way fabrics Fabrics that have a nap or a special print, and thus must be cut in one direction only.

pinking Finishing an edge with pinking shears, which produces a zigzag cut and prevents many fabrics from fraying. This is the easiest way to finish a seam.

presser foot The changeable device on a sewing machine that holds the fabric in place during sewing. Special presser feet are required for specific tasks such as sewing a zipper.

raglan sleeve A sleeve joined to the body of a garment by a diagonal seam starting at the neckline.

right side/wrong side The right side of fabric is the side designed to be seen. The wrong side is the "back." However, you may choose to use the wrong side as a design accent, or even make a garment with the wrong side out. If so, designate it the "right" side for the purposes of the instructions in this book. Pieces are often sewn "face to face," which means right side to right side.

rotary cutter and mat A wheel-shaped blade used to cut pattern pieces quickly and efficiently with less strain on the wrist. Must be used with a self-healing mat to prevent damage to the surface beneath.

seam A line of stitching that joins two pieces of fabric.

seam allowance The area in between the edge of the cut piece and the line where the seam is stitched. Seam allowances are not built into the patterns in this book and must be added before finalizing each design's pattern.

seam ripper A small tool used to tear open seams without cutting into fabric.

self The primary fabric used for the outside of a dress; as opposed to the lining, interfacing, or trim.

selvage The finished side edges of a bolt of fabric.

serger A type of sewing machine that uses multiple spools of thread to sew, trim, and finish seams simultaneously. Used to make professional-quality knits. Not for beginners.

set-in sleeve A standard sleeve that is joined to the body of the garment by a seam starting at the shoulder and continuing around the armhole.

shank The stem of a button.

slashing and spreading In patternmaking, a cutting and expanding technique for making a pattern larger from within, rather than adding to hems or side seams, to preserve its outermost measurements.

sloper A basic pattern, without seam allowances, from which individual dress style patterns are adapted.

staystitch A basting stitch applied along the seam allowance. Sewn to a piece before joining it to another piece to stabilize delicate areas and prevent stretching.

style lines Seams that exist for decorative, rather than structural, purposes, such as to create the illusion of a bustier or for color-blocking.

thread tension The balance between the needle and bobbin threads in a stitch. If one of the threads pulls with more tension than the other, the stitch will not meet in the center of the fabric. Must be calibrated before sewing a garment.

topstitch A stitch sewn about ¼" (6mm) from seam allowance edge, with the right side of fabric facing up during sewing. Can be functional or decorative.

understitch When a seam allowance is folded over and hidden inside facing, this stitch joins the seam allowance to the facing. The wrong side of fabric faces up during sewing.

Biographies

warp Also known as the lengthwise grain or grainline. Runs parallel to selvage and is the strongest direction of the fabric.

weft Also known as the crosswise grain. Runs from selvage to selvage.

yoke A shaped panel of fabric that is topstitched onto or inserted into a garment for decorative or shaping purposes.

zigzag stitch A z-shaped stitch that allows for more stretch and is thus used for knits. Tight zigzag stitches form buttonholes and appliqué borders.

Wendy Mullin

Wendy Mullin is the designer behind the label Built by Wendy, established in 1991. She is a self-taught sewer and patternmaker with over 25 years of experience. She lives and works in New York City. For more information about Wendy, visit her website, www.builtbywendy.com

Eviana Hartman

Collaborating with Wendy on the writing of *Sew U* editions made Eviana Hartman so excited about sewing that she started her own clothing line, Bodkin, in 2008. Hartman was previously an eco-columnist for the *Washington Post*, the fashion features editor at *NYLON*, and a fashion writer at *Vogue* and *Teen Vogue*, and has also written for *Dwell*, *I.D.*, *Purple Fashion*, and *Wired*. She lives in Brooklyn, New York and also plays drums and keyboards in an as-yet-unnamed band.

Beci Orpin

Beci Orpin is a designer-illustrator based in Melbourne, Australia. She has been working freelance for over 10 years and her clients include Universal Music, Visa, Foster's and Mercedes-Benz. Beci also exhibits her work frequently and runs children's clothing label Tiny Mammoth. When she is not working, Beci likes riding her bike, gardening, and hanging out with her two sons Tyke and Ari, and partner Raph. For more information about Beci, visit her website at www.beciorpin.com

Dana Vaccarelli

Dana Vaccarelli graduated from the School of Visual Arts in 2007, and works as a graphic designer at Built by Wendy in NYC. She loves her job, but admits that she's mainly in it for the clothes. For more about Dana, you may visit her website www.danavaccarelli.com.

Index

A

About a Boy dress, 135–139
Afternoon Delight dress, 173
A-line hem, 23
A Little Romance dress, 151
altering, 36–37, 203
American Pastoral dress, 154–157
appliqué, 26
athletic figure, 17
average figure, 17

B

Baja Fresh pullover, 106–110
Ballerina Girl dress, 113
banded hem, 23
bateau neckline, 18
batiste, 24
bell sleeve, 21
bias binding, 65
blended fabrics, 25
blindstitch hem, 66
Bohemian Rhapsody dress, 176–180
Bold Shoulders dress, 145–148
Bow Wow dress, 102–105
boy figure, 16
broadcloth, 24
buttonholes, 68
buttons, 26, 68–69

C

Cannes Do dress, 87–91
canvas, 25
Capri Sundress, 83–86
cap sleeve, 20
changing fit, 203
charmeuse, 25
Chelsea collar, 19
chiffon, 25
classic hem, 22
closures, 26
collars, 19
Color Purple dress, 183

colors, 27
convertible collar, 19
cordage, 26
cotton, 24–25
crepe, 25
crepe de Chine, 25
cuffs, 21
curved seams, 58–59
cutting, 50–51

D

darts, 34
deconstruction, 203
Deep Impact dress, 127–130
dirndl dress, 15
dirndl hem, 23
drawstring dress, 92–96

E

edgestitching, 61
elastic cuff, 21
Empress dress, 167

F

fabrics, 24–25
facings, 63–64
Fiesta dress, 198
figure types, 16–17
fray-proofing, 60
French curve, 31
French Sailor dress, 123–126
Frill Seeker dress, 133
full hem, 22

G

gathered seams, 59
gauze, 24
G.I. Jane dress, 80
Girls Will Be Girls dress, 137
grain lines, 35

H

Hello, Sailor! dress, 178
hem finishing, 66
hems, 22–23, 66
herringbone, 25
Hipper Zipper jumper, 125

Hothouse Flowers dress, 191–195
hourglass figure, 17

I

Into the Woods dress, 155
iron, 56

L

La Boheme dress, 85
lace, 26
lawn cotton, 24
linings, 25, 65
Lolita dress, 181–185
long sleeve, 20
Lumberjack dress, 165–169
Luxe Be a Lady dress, 129

M

mandarin collar, 19
markers, 47
maxi hem, 22
measuring, 32–33
measuring tape, 31
mini hem, 22
Mod World dress, 104
muslin test garment, 38–42

N

necklines, 18–19
needles, 55
notches, 35

O

Oktober dress, 111–115
Overall Improvement jumper, 97–101

P

Palm Beach tunic, 118–122
paper, 31
Parachute dress, 149–153
pear figure, 16
pencil, 31
pencil hem, 23
Peter Pan collar, 19
pinking shears, 60
pins, 47, 55
piping, 26

piqué, 25
pockets, 72–75
preshrinking, 48
prints, 27
puff sleeve, 21

R

repurposing fabric, 203
rhinestones, 26
ribbons, 26
rickrack, 26
ripper, 55
Rock the Boatneck dress, 131–134
rolled cuff, 21
ruffle collar, 19
ruffle cuff, 21
ruffled hem, 23
ruler, 31

S

scissors, 31, 47, 55
scoop neckline, 18
Sea Change dress, 108
seam allowances, 34
seam ripper, 55
seams, 58–59
serger, 56, 60
sewing machine, 56
sheath dress, 15
Sheer Genius dress, 142
shift dress, 15
shirt cuff, 21
shirt tail hem, 23
Shooting Star dress, 162
short sleeve, 20
sides, of fabric, 48
silk, 25
sizing, 32–33
sleeveless, 20
sleeves, 20–21
sloper set, 43
snaps, 26
square neckline, 19
straight pins, 55
sweetheart neckline, 19

T

tape, 31
Tea dress, 186–190
tea hem, 22
Tennis Anyone? dress, 196–200
That's a Wrap dress, 194
thread, 55
three quarter sleeve, 20
tie collar, 19
Too Cool for School dress, 99
tools, 31
topstitched hem, 66
topstitching, 61
tracing wheel, 31
trims, 26, 67
trueing patterns, 43
tunic hem, 23
tweed, 25
twill, 25
Two-Tone tunic, 120

U

understitching, 61
U-neck, 18
Uptown Girl dress, 160–164
Urban Peasant dress, 89
Use Your Illusion dress, 140–144

V

Valentine dress, 170–175
V 2.0 dress, 188
V-neck, 18
voile, 25

W

weight, fabric, 27
weights, 47
wool, 25
Workin' Nine to Five dress, 78–82

Z

zigzag stitch, 60
zippers, 26, 70–71